Karl Kautsky

LIVES of the LEFT is a new series of original biographies of leading figures in the European and North American socialist and labour movements. Short, lively and accessible they will be welcomed by students of history and politics and by anyone interested in the development of the Left.   *general editor*   David Howell

published: **J. Ramsay MacDonald**   Austen Morgan
James Maxton   William Knox
Karl Kautsky Dick Geary

forthcoming, to include: **Big Bill Haywood**   Melvin Dubofsky
A. J. Cook   Paul Davies
Aneurin Bevan   Dai Smith
Thomas Johnston   Graham Walker
Eugene Debs   Gail Malmgreen
R. H. Tawney   Anthony Wright
Ernest Bevin   Peter Weiler

Karl Kautsky

Dick Geary

Manchester University Press

Published by Manchester University Press, Oxford Road,
Manchester, M13 9PL, UK

British Library cataloguing in publication data

Geary, Dick
    Karl Kautsky. —(Lives of the left; 1)
    1. Kautsky, Karl
    I. Title   II. Series
    335.4'092'4   HX273.K34

ISBN 0 7190 2158 8 *hardback*
ISBN 0 7190 2159 6 *paper*

Printed and bound in Great Britain by
Robert Hartnoll (1985) Ltd., Bodmin, Cornwall

Contents

Preface

Karl Kautsky was the leading interpreter of Marx after the death of Engels. To a generation of Marxist intellectuals, including Luxemburg, Lenin and Trotsky, he was mentor and was widely regarded by German Social Democrats and other members of the Second International as the 'Pope' of Socialism – an intentionally ambiguous accolade. His importance stems less from significantly novel contributions to Marxist theory, though in the areas of revolutionary consciousness and concepts of Imperialism Kautsky *did* make important contributions, than in his spirited defence and elucidation of the original theory and in the nature of his popularisation/vulgarisation thereof. It is his *mis*reading of Marx which is often the crucial point. Finally it was through a critique of Kautskyite theory that younger Marxists, such as Lenin, Luxemburg and Lukacs, came to develop a new revolutionary strategy.

This work rests on a study of the massively numerous publications of Kautsky and unpublished materials, primarily in the International Institute for Social History in Amsterdam. The format of the series in which the present work appears prevents the detailed citation of articles and letters. For references, therefore, readers should consult my Ph.D (*Karl Kautsky and the Development of Marxism,* University of Cambridge, 1971), which also contains a lengthy bibliography of both Kautsky's own work and of the secondary literature.

I should like to express my thanks to the staff of the Institute for Social History for their help and kindness, to David McLellan,

Karl Kautsky

Hans-Josef Steinberg and, above all, to my former research supervisors Ted (E. H.) Carr and Jonathan Steinberg.

Lancaster 1985

1 Introduction

Karl Marx died in 1883. He bequeathed the most ambitious and impressive intellectual legacy to posterity. Yet that theory had only the most tenuous hold on a minute section of the European Labour movement in the early 1880s. In Britain, organised labour was to be a source of despair to Engels on account of its reformist politics, giving rise to the concept of a 'labour aristocracy' bought off by high wages and the profits of empire. In Germany, the emergence of independent working-class political parties in the 1860s had not taken place under a Marxist banner either. In the 1860s the main debate had been between liberal theories of working-class self-help (Schulze-Delitzsch and Sonnemann) on the one hand and various theories of 'State-Socialism' (Rodbertus, Dühring, Lassalle) on the other. The emergence of Lassalle's General Union of German Workers in 1863, and subsequently of the Eisenach party of August Bebel and Wilhelm Liebknecht, did not initially make for theoretical clarity. It is quite misleading to view the one party as 'Lassallean' and the other as 'Marxist' for, as Susanne Miller, Roger Morgan and Detlef Lehnert have shown, both organisations were extremely eclectic, not to say confused, in their views to the mid-1870s and beyond. The Gotha Programme of 1875, drawn up when the two parties united to form what subsequently became known as the Social Democratic Party (SPD) and which earned the scathing critique of Marx himself, was not a trade-off between Lassalleans and Marxists but a testimony to precisely that confusion.

Slowly but surely, however, certain historical events served to prepare the ground for a more general reception of Marxist theory. The process of industrialisation was not least important in this regard. In 1846 all Prussian territories produced less coal than London alone consumed. By 1870 production had risen to twenty nine million tons a year and twenty years later the figure had reached seventy million tons. Urbanisation on a spectacular and rapid scale accompanied industrialisation. In 1871 sixty four per cent of the Reich's population lived in rural areas. By 1900 only forty five per cent did so. Factories increasingly replaced the domestic worker and the craftsman; between 1882 and 1892 alone the average number of employees per firm doubled in the German cotton industry.

The concentration of capital also seemed to be following the Marxian prognosis, at least in some industrial sectors, with the emergence of the chemical and electrical giants (Bayer, BASF, AEG and Siemens), of gigantic empires in coal, iron and steel (Thyssen, Krupp and Stumm) and huge pits on the Ruhr. The new and increasingly concentrated industrial labour force also had to undergo several other processes foreseen by Marx, including economic depression. The extent to which there really was a 'great depression' between 1873 and 1896 is of course a source of dispute amongst economic historians but there is no doubt that many contemporaries, amongst them August Bebel and Eduard Bernstein, (initially), saw the recession as nothing less than the 'final crisis of Capitalism'. Certainly the 1870s witnessed significant levels of both unemployment in the producer-goods sector and working-class insecurity.

Certain economic developments thus seemed to verify aspects of Marx's view and prepared the way for the reception of 'Scientific Socialism'. However, the adoption of Marxism by a significant section of the German Labour movement was no mechanical consequence of industrialisation. As I have argued elsewhere, even more important was the role of the German state. Discriminatory taxation and tariff policies, the unequal suffrages of the most important of the *Länder* and the absence of parliamentary sovereignty all exposed the class nature of the Prusso-German state. Above all, the actual repression of working-class organisations, especially, but not only, during the years of the notorious 'Anti-Socialist Law' (1878-90) when the SPD was outlawed, served to radicalise Labour politics and coincided with the adoption of Marxism as the official theory of German Social Democracy at the Erfurt Congress of 1891.

To a certain extent, therefore, the reception of a radical Socialist doctrine in Germany in the 1880s amd thereafter was a consequence of the combined factors of depression and repression. However, the fact that it was a specifically *Marxist* theory which benefitted from this conjuncture was far from a simple consequence of economic and political developments. Marx's writings were difficult, diffuse, had appeared in many languages and were not widely read in Germany. What was needed was a systematic popularisation of his theories and it was this task which Friedrich Engels took upon himself, in works such as *Anti-Dühring,* published in book form in 1878. This work had an enormous impact on German Socialists, and in particular on two young men who were to play a major role in the dissemination of Marxism: Eduard Bernstein and Karl Kautsky. Together with, and under the guidance of, Engels they propagated the new ideas in journals such as the *Sozialdemokrat,* published in exile in Zürich and distributed illegally within Germany during the Anti-Socialist Law, and later in *Die Neue Zeit.* It was in fact they who drew up the Erfurt Programme in 1891. Kautsky was responsible for the first part of that programme which outlined the general development of capitalist society (social polarisation, increasing class conflict and socialisation of the means of production as the long-term goal) in a Marxist fashion, whilst Bernstein wrote the second 'minimum' programme, which consisted of short-term demands for democratic reform and improvements in working conditions.

Eduard Bernstein was born in 1850, the seventh son of a Jewish engine driver. Largely self-taught and finding employment as a bank clerk, he was first attracted to German Social Democracy by its opposition to the annexation of Alsace-Lorraine in the wake of the Franco-Prussian war. With the onset of the Anti-Socialist Law in 1878, which made membership of the SPD illegal and drove many socialists into exile, Bernstein travelled to Zürich as private secretary to Karl Höchberg, who there edited journals which were smuggled illegally into the German Reich. Whilst in Zürich he got to know Karl Kautsky and, together with his younger colleague and under the influence of Engels, Bernstein played a major role in the propagation of Marxism. It was only later, in the second half of the 1890s, that he began to question the major tenets of that theory and became the best known of all the 'revisionists'. Karl Kautsky came from a somewhat more exalted and bohemian background. He was born in Prague in 1854, son of an artist father and a mother who was first an actress but then took to writing widely-read Socialist novels *(Stefan von Grillenhof, Die Alten und die Neuen, Herrschen oder Dienen)* which were also much admired by Engels. At around the age of twenty, after studying history and the natural sciences at the Universty of Vienna, Kautsky became active in the Austrian Socialist movement and began to write in its journals. Attempts to earn a living as an artist or actor came to nothing and, although a play of Kautsky's was once performed in Vienna in 1878, a novel he had written remained unpublished. At much the same time Kautsky had begun to write articles for the Socialist press in Leipzig and had come into contact with the leaders of the German Labour movement. From 1879 he began work on Höchberg's newspaper, *Der Sozialdemokrat,* in Zürich, where he met and was greatly influenced by Eduard Bernstein, four years his senior. From this time on Kautsky devoted his time and energy to the service of German Social Democracy, travelling to London in 1881 to meet Marx and Engels for the first time. He spent a further five years in the English capital between 1885 and 1890, remaining in close touch with Engels, with whom he always got on better than with Marx. In the meantime he launched what was to become the most prestigious of all international Marxist journals, *Die Neue Zeit (The New Age),* in 1883. Ironically this task was made easier by the Prussian censor, who banned much overtly subversive literature but was not offended by the tone of 'scientific' seriousness adopted in that journal. *Die Neue Zeit,* of which Kautsky remained editor until 1917, created his national and international reputation as an expounder of Marx. He became the SPD's 'party professor', as the Bavarian Socialist leader Georg von Vollmar ironically remarked, and the most revered theorist of the Second International, an international federation of nationally-based Socialist parties founded in Paris in 1889.

Kautsky's rise to prominence amongst the ranks of Marxist intellectualls owed more to the power and presence of his own party organisation, the German Social Democratric Party, within the Second International than to intellectual fireworks on his part, for the SPD emerged in the two decades before the First World War as the largest Socialist party in the world. After managing to survive the persecution of the Anti-Socialist Law (1878-90) the SPD went on to build a massive organisational empire, with a veritable army of paid funtionaries. It published over seventy newspapers and provided a range of facilities, including insurance schemes and advice on legal issues affecting workers. The party also ran a host of ancillary organisations, including gymnastics associations, choral societies, soccer, stamp-collecting, educational associations, cyclist organisations and even smoking (!) clubs. A veritable sub-culture was created in the large industrial cities of Protestant Germany. (Significantly the SPD always had difficulty in mobilising the support of Catholics, even in industrial areas.) By 1914 the SPD had over one million individual due-paying members, of whom between eighty and ninety five per cent were manual workers, albeit overwhelmingly from the skilled trades. (The unskilled, casually employed, Catholics, Poles and women workers were notable for their absence from the ranks.) The voting strength of the party was even more impressive. In the Reichstag elections of 1877 the SPD gained 9.1% of the total vote cast, 23.3% in 1893 and 34.8% in 1912. In that last year over four million Germans gave their electoral support to Social Democracy, which was well on its way to monopolising the Labour vote in the large Protestant towns.

This apparent success, however, serves to hide two crucial points. Despite its electoral strength, the SPD was no nearer political power in 1912 than in 1893, simply because the constitutional system placed real power outside the hands of the elected representatives in the Reichstag. No Social Democrat was included in government, even at a regional or local level, before 1918. What is more, it was not only urban Socialists who turned out at the polls in ever increasing numbers in Imperial Germany. Political mobilisation of the masses was a universal phenomenon in the Second Reich after 1890; in the first national elections of 1871 approximately fifty per cent of the German electorate turned out to vote. In 1907 and 1912 the figure was in the order of eighty five per cent. Many of these new voters from non-proletarian strata formed the backbone of reaction and the more the SPD vote grew, the more an anti-Socialist neurosis forced the other interests together. In this context the SPD was isolated and effectively impotent. Any attempt to mount the barricades would lead to annihilation, whilst the prospect of an alliance with supposedly 'progressive' elements of the bourgeoisie was equally remote. The subsequent chapters of this book will argue that it was precisely this situation which rendered Rosa Luxemburg's revolutionaly dreams utopian and Eduard Bernstein's vision of a gradual transition to Socialism illusory in Germany before the First World War. The passivity and inadequacies of Kautsky's political thought, on the other hand, both made sense of and can be explained by this stalemate in the German political scene before 1914.

A second fact which rendered the SPD's threat to the existing political and social order of Wilhelmine Germany less real than was often imagined was the existence of marked divisions within the party itself. At Gotha in 1875 the newly united Social-Democratic movement incorporated several inchoate and conflicting theoretical positions. The years of persecution between 1873 and 1890 did serve to bring about a greater degree of unity within the party and formed the backcloth for the adoption of Marxism as the official party ideology at Erfurt in 1891. However, even in the years of the anti-socialist law, there were those who advocated piecemeal change within the existing order. This was especially so within the ranks of the SPD Reichstag *Fraktion* (parliamentary delegation) and became clear in a debate on the question of subsidising German colonial steamship lines in 1884-5. After 1890 the trade-union wing of the party, which became especially strong as the membership of the Free Trade Unions eclipsed that of the SPD after 1902 (reaching 2.6 million in 1914), ceaselessly advocated caution, counselled against political strikes and generally looked to reformist solutions to the problems of working-class daily existence. The very creation of the party bureaucracy may also have fuelled caution and conservatism; though, as I have argued elsewhere, this process is easily exaggerated. In the South German States, especially Baden, a relatively liberal constitution produced a section of the SPD which did believe in class collaboration and reform within the prevailing order. Yet, again as I have argued at length elsewhere, such reformism made little sense to the largest Social-Democratic branches in Prussia, Saxony and Hamburg, where discriminatory franchises and an increasingly reactionary bourgeoisie paved the way for the politics of class isolationism, which again found expression in Kautsky's thinking. There did exist places where the local SPD was committed to radical and revolutionary politics, as in parts of Berlin, Bremen, Brunswick. Remscheid, Solingen, Stuttgart, Göppingen and Düsseldorf.

The fact that German Social Democracy comprised such disparate elements explains the heated debates which characterised its existence. In those debates Kautsky often played a leading role. In the 1880s it was Kautsky, together with Engels and Bernstein and with the help of the charismatic party leader August Bebel, who drove the malignant 'State-Socialist' ideas of Rodbertus, Dühring and Lassalle out of the party (or, in the latter case, at least underground). In this period Kautsky was also concerned to demonstrate that the social legislation introduced by Bismarck would make little difference to the worker's existence and could not obviate the need for social revolution. It was in these years that Kautsky made Marxism the official ideology of a mass movement. In the early 1890s the SPD was confronted by the continued existence of a large land-owning peasantry in South Germany. This led some within the party, such as the South-German revisionist Eduard David, but also even the party-leader Bebel, to advocate a specifically agrarian strategy for the party, intended to win peasant votes through a policy of peasant protection. It was Kautsky who led the assault on this proposed strategy at the 1895 party congress, though his success at that congress arguably had more to do with the fact that the SPD was overwhelmingly a party of urban consumers than with any innate theoretical superiority. In the late 1890s, this time with the full support of Bebel, Kautsky led the orthodox attack on the ideas of his former friend (and one-time Marxist) Bernstein, who came to criticise various aspects of the Marxian prognosis, such as the theories of crisis, impoverishment and class polarisation, in the light of the economic recovery of the late 1890s and the ending of the Anti-Socialist Law. Again Kautsky was successful, for 're-visionist' ideas were overwhelmingly rejected at the party conference of 1903 in Dresden, though again it was the political realities of Imperial Germany which gave his arguments succour. He played an equally prominent part in the mass-strike debates of 1905-12, supporting the concept in principle but coming out very strongly against the advocates of its use in Germany, such as Rosa Luxemburg and Anton Pannekoek. On the outbreak of the First World War Kautsky advocated that the SPD abstain from voting for the government war credits and by 1915 was opposing the annexationist aims of the Reich and advocating peace. Finally, and perhaps most notoriously, it was the sixty-three year old Social Democrat who took up his pen to write against Bolshevik revolutionary practice in 1917-18 and who proclaimed Lenin's betrayal of Socialism in his work on the *Dictatorship of the Proletariat.*

By the time of the outbreak of the First World War, however, Kautsky's reputation was already sinking. In his early struggles against reformists and revisionists he had been able to rely on the support of the Marxist left (Luxemburg, Pannekoek, Parvus and Lenin). His restraint on the issue of the mass strike, however and the adumbration of the theory of 'Ultra-imperialism' after 1911, which stated that Capitalist Imperialism would not necessarily lead to war, left Kautsky and the so-called 'centre' increasingly isolated. The SPD's support for the German war effort discredited that party, and with it Kautsky, in the eyes of Lenin and the revolutionary left. The split of the party into two wings in 1917, which was much to Kautsky's distaste, despite his opposition to the war effort and thus to the majority position in the SPD, led to the formation of the Independent Social Democratic Party (USPD) in which Kautsky found himself. It also, however, led to his loss of the editorship of *Die Neue Zeit,* his major platform.

Henceforth in a period of revolutionary upheaval, and one in which the Labour movement split into Social-Democratic and Communist wings, Kautsky became an increasingly marginal figure, rejoining the SPD in 1922. He was now reviled by Communists as the counter-revolutionary critic of Lenin, who had, after all, presided over a successful revolution; and although he was to draft the SPD's Heidelberg Programme of 1925, he could never really feel at home in the increasingly reformist party in the Weimar Republic. In a sense Kautsky's theory had been one suited to Imperial Germany, but not to the upheavals and missed opportunities of the post-war era. In 1924 he went to Vienna, where his three sons lived, on the invitation of the Austrian Socialists. There he had to witness the defeat of German Socialism at the hands of Hitler and the annihilation of Austrian Social Democracy in the civil war of 1934. That 'optimistic fatalism' which was the hallmark of Kautskyite political theory ('history is on our side') still surfaced in his publications of 1934, as in his pamphlet *Grenzen der Gewalt (The Limits of Force),* but was clearly historically redundant. In this sense at least Trotsky was right when he declared that Kautsky had been condemned to the rubbish heap of history. On the German annexation of Austria, the aged theorist, whose works had long been banned by the Nazis, fled by aeroplane to Amsterdam where he died on 17 October 1938.

The intellectual history of Marxism between the death of Marx and the outbreak of the First World War cannot ignore the figure of Kautsky. Only two Marxist works circulated widely in Imperial Germany: Bebel's *Die Frau und der Sozialismus (Woman and Socialism)* and Kautsky's *Die Ökonomischen Lehren von Karl Marx (Marx's Economic Doctrines).* Lenin, Luxemburg, Trotsky, Guesde and innumerable Marxists of the Second International either came to Marx through Kautsky's writings or relied on him for advice. All corresponded with him. However, to say that Kautsky is an important figure in intellectual history is not to say that his theories had an especial impact on the rank and file of the German Labour movement. The work of Steinberg, Langewiesche and Schönhoven has shown that few Social Democrats actually visited the lending libraries of the party or the Free Trade Unions. Those that did more usually borrowed works of fiction (especially the historical novels of Alexandre Dumas) rather than non-fiction; and what non-fiction was read was a mixture of vocational training and evolutionary biology. Even the leadership of the SPD was arguably more influenced by popularisations of evolutionary biology (often transposed onto the social sciences) than the difficult writings of Marx. In any case, some sections of the party revealed a pronounced distaste for *any* form of theoretical controversy, whether generated by revisionists or Marxists. Thus the trade-union leader Robert Schmidt, who was certainly no friend of the left, berated Bernstein for stirring up unnecessary dissension, as did the reformist Bavarian Georg von Vollmar and the influential pragmatist and leading party member Ignaz Auer. This is not to say that the SPD lacked members who were committed to revolutionary change. Indeed, I have argued at length elsewhere that there is a radical continuity which spans the war in some parts of Germany. But the precise significance of Marxist *theory* for that radicalism is more than a little debatable. Significantly many of the most important reformists in the party refused to support Bernstein at party conferences. However, not the least reason for this is precisely that Kautsky's work reflected the isolation and impotence of Social Democracy in Wilhelmine Germany. The promise of social revolution yet almost total silence on questions of daily tactics which characterised 'centrism' could in fact keep most people happy. The revolutionary rhetoric suited the left, whilst the day-to-day struggles of the reformists could continue unimpeded. Only in a genuinely revolutionary situation at the end of the First World War were the contradictions inherent in this position cruelly exposed.

In the various controversies mentioned above, Kautsky's arguments invariably centered upon an analysis of the present and not moral categories. Such disputes over the appropriate strategy for the attainment of Socialism stemmed less from moral judgements concerning the use of violence than from different analyses of the need for and consequences of its use in bourgeois society. For Kautsky, Socialism was not a question of ethics, of moral choice, but a 'science', the outcome of a correct analysis of the Capitalist mode of production and its consequences. In fact 'Utopian Socialism', neo-Kantianism and any other ethical formulation of Socialism were anathema to him and his opposition to revisionism stemmed not least from this. (Bernstein, as Roger Fletcher has pointed out, was not, strictly speaking, a neo-Kantian, though other revisionists, such as Kurt Eisner, were. However, Bernstein did share with other revisionists a scepticism towards claims of 'scientific' accuracy on the part of theorists such as Kautsky.) For the latter, any correct Socialist position had to be erected on an accurate analysis of Capitalism, not upon pious wishes. Socialist theory had to serve the needs of a mass political movement. It could not be relegated to the realm of individual moral choice. By this, Kautsky did not mean that moral judgements were irrelevant for a Marxist. He spoke of the struggle against inequality as part of man's 'moral nature'. On occasion he even admitted that the categorical imperative might serve as a formulation of the socialist aim to end all exploitation. It was just that on its own it could not serve as the basis of Socialist theory. Plekhanov and Pannekoek both detected Kautsky's difficulties over this issue and he himself was forced to admit in a letter to the former that philosophy had never been his 'strong point' (letter of 22 May 1898).

Kautsky's opposition to ethical formulations of the Socialist ideal rested primarily on the practical consequences of such a position rather than the philosophical niceties. He realised that Bernstein's position implied that Socialism did not have to be class-based; for if it were a matter of individual conscience, and not the outcome of the objective interests of a particular class in Capitalist society, then there was no reason to believe in either the inevitability of its triumph or that policy of proletarian isolation, which, as we will see, was the cornerstone of Kautsky's political thinking. He was well aware of, and especially disturbed by, the connection between an ethical formulation of Socialism and the advocacy of reconciliation with progressive sections of the bourgeoisie. Indeed, this was precisely why he maintained that revisionism implied a change in the established isolationist strategy of the SPD. For him, ethical judgements were both historically determined and class-specific. Each class possessed its own distinct ethic and only the proletariat in Capitalist society could be truly Socialist.

The basis of Kautsky's socialist commitment, in his own mind, was the correct analysis of the mechanics of Capitalist society. From this analysis, and not from that of past revolutions, he constructed his model of the impending social revolution. In fact, he explicitly condemned those who sought guidance from the past, including Engels, who, in Kautsky's opinion, had been misled by taking the Jacobin experience as his model. This also explains his unwillingness – in contradistinction to his younger Polish colleague, Rosa Luxemburg – to draw conclusions for German revolutionary practice from the events of 1905 and 1917 in Russia. For him, as for many of his Socialist contemporaries, the naïve enthusiasm for direct action and the general strike was anachronistic in the German situation. Russia was simply an 'immature' and 'backward' society.

For Kautsky it was the German present, not Russia or the past, which supplied the key to the coming revolution. Hence his theory of social revolution centered on an analysis of the contradictions of his own environment. His analysis of those contradictions was most certainly not original. Most of it was lifted from the works of Marx, in particular from *Das Kapital,* and even more from those of Engels – a debt which Kautsky was of course the first to acknowledge. In many ways his work is best described as a popularisation of the work of these masters. Yet it would be a mistake to think that the SPD's leading theorist merely regurgitated the work of others. At times, as in his development of the theory of revolutionary consciousness ('consciousness from without') and his many – often contradictory – theories of Imperialism, Kautsky made a meaningful and independent contribution to Marxist theory. He did far more than simply 'add' to the work of Marx, however. As the theorist of a mass political party and one who wrote for six decades following Marx's death, he was required to apply Marxist theories to the exigencies of SPD party politics and to the situation in Wilhelmine (and subsequently Weimar) Germany. In so doing, Kautsky transformed the original theory and bestowed new meanings on well-worn phrases. In this sense, though certainly not intentionally, Kautsky too was a 'revisionist'.

2 Class conflict and Capitalist crisis

For Kautsky, following Marx, Capitalist society was characterised by 'commodity production', production for 'exchange not use', a highly developed division of labour and the predominance of industry over other sectors of the economy. The division of labour, which primarily rested upon private ownership of the means of production, produced different and competing classes in a society rent with class conflict. Kautsky was perfectly aware that conflicts within Capitalist society could not simply be reduced to a single dichotomy of industrial Capitalist versus industrial wage-labourer. He paid especial attention to what he saw as an inevitable conflict between the urban worker and that throwback to a former age, the German peasant, for example. The protection of the peasant smallholding, argued Kautsky, meant a rise in food prices for the urban consumer, as did a tariff policy directed against the import of foreign agricultural products. (This was a programme which the SPD was to use with enormous success in election afer election; the price of food to the German worker was determined less by market forces than the policies of the Wilhelmine state.) In addition, the peasantry had a vested interest in the maintenance of private ownership. Although it might on occasion be mobilised against the interests of large landowners, it could never be Socialist in its commitment. As a result, Kautsky launched a bitter polemic against those in his party, including initially the party leader Bebel but more especially Eduard David and the South German reformists, who advocated a policy of peasant protection in order to win peasant votes. For Kautsky, the best the party could do was to 'neutralise' the peasantry. It would never be an ally for the Socialist reconstruction of society. (That this line proved dominant within German Social Democracy before the First World War was simply a reflection of the fact that the SPD's membership was up to 90% industrial working-class, was overwhelmingly concentrated in the large industrial cities of Protestant Germany (Berlin, Hamburg and Leipzig). In 1900 the Berlin party branch had at least as many members as all the party branches south of the River Main put together.)

There could be no doubt in Kautsky's mind, however, that the sharpest and most significant clash of interests in Capitalist society was that between industrial capital and industrial labour. This was a conflict beyond reconciliation and one which would prove decisive for the future shape of society. The irreconcilability of interests stemmed from the private ownership of the means of production, the fact that capital was concentrated in a few hands and the consequence that profit, not use, was the motive force of Capitalism. As a result, the Capitalist mode of production necessarily entailed the exploitation of wage-labour according to the theory of surplus value, as adumbrated by Marx. Kautsky was committed to this theory as early as 1880 but could still write in 1925: 'For that value which Marx and classical economy had in mind, no determining factor other than labour has yet been found. The theory of labour-value has stood the test.'[1] According to this theory (in Kautsky's version), the profits on which industrial entrepreneurs built their fortunes were derived from surplus value, which itself 'arises from the fact that the entrepreneur forces the workers to work longer than is necessary for the reproduction of their wages. This surplus labour constitutes the surplus value.'[2] As profit was the whole point of commodity production and as the industrialist could only survive by continuously accumulating capital, so the Capitalist mode of production could not fail to rest upon the exploitation of the working class.

Kautsky's repetition of this central category of Marxian economics was no mere academic exercise. It was this analysis which informed the central notion of Kautskyite political thinking: the class-based nature of socialism and the doctrine of proletarian isolation. He rejected all moves to transform the SPD from a *Klassenpartei* (class-based party) into a more broadly-based *Volkspartei,* as advocated by the reformist and revisionist wings of the movement. For him, the SPD had to be committed to the principle of class conflict, the starting-point for all Socialist thought and action. The idea that a party might represent bourgeois and proletarian interests simultaneously was simply rubbish. Above all, the Labour movement had to remain *independent,* had to make every effort to distinguish itself from Liberalism. In Kautsky's mind a strong Labour movement and a flourishing Liberalism were incompatible. Alliances with middle-class Liberals, who in any case were moving increasingly to the right in alliance with the forces of Militarism and Imperialism, were to be avoided and could achieve nothing of lasting value. Only the interests of the proletariat, the propertyless class, coincided with the principle of socialisation of the means of production; and so the SPD must remain a party of urban workers and the working class would have to make the social revolution unaided. Nothing was 'to be gained from collaboration with the existing order. 'To tell the proletariat to abandon the class struggle is to recommend to it unconditional submission to the commands of capital,' wrote Kautsky in 1917.[3] The same theme had been central to Kautsky's opposition to revisionism, as we will see.

The adoption of such arguments by the editor of *Die Neue Zeit* was scarcely surprising, given the political situation of Imperial Germany, where a substantial section of the industrial élite had thrown in its lot with the semi-autocratic governmental system, where the Liberal movement was relatively weak, where employers refused to recognise unions and where parts of the lower middle class of artisans, small shop-keepers and independent peasant farmers were already mobilised in anti-Labour alliances, such as the *Kartell der schaffenden Stände* (cartel of productive estates), known to Social Democrats as the *Kartell der raffenden Hände* (cartel of grasping hands). Independence and isolation in such a hostile environment was an article of faith not only for Kautsky, but also for August Bebel and Rosa Luxemburg. The importance attached to the issue by Social Democrats more generally is revealed by events at the Dresden Party Conference of 1903, when virtually the biggest single issue – despite the fact that this was the conference which debated the revisionist heresy and condemned Bernstein – was the question of whether party members should contribute to the bourgeois press!

As class conflicts were 'in the last resort' conflicts of interest, so Kautsky believed that they could not be resolved by argument and gentle persuasion. And as only proletarian interests were in keeping with the Socialist reconstruction of society, so Kautsky was forced to speak out against the revisionist ideas of Bernstein and proclaim the necessity of the dictatorship of the proletariat. What Kautsky meant by this concept, however, may come as something of a surprise. He did not necessarily equate it with the forcible expropriation of the bourgeoisie or autocratic rule. This of course became clear in his critique of the Bolshevik Revolution when he claimed – with good reason – that Marx had not used the term dictatorship in its literal sense. Marx had referred not to a specific form of government but to a situation in which the working class, or rather its representatives, ruled on their own (i.e. not in alliance with other classes). Kautsky pointed out that Marx and Engels had seen the Paris Commune of 1871 as a model for such dictatorship and that the Commune had rested on a system of direct elections and universal suffrage. It is important to realise that this diluted democratic interpretation of proletarian dictorship was *not* the fruit of an increasingly conservative old age. In this respect, as Salvadori has argued, Kautsky did not change his mind. In one of his earliest full-length works, published in 1893, Kautsky had already written that parliamentary democracy could as easily be a tool of the working class as of the bourgeoisie. He said much the same in a letter of the same year to party comrade Franz Mehring who subsequently became a founder member of the KPD. Hence it is not so surprising that Vladimir Akimov, a Russian Social Democratic (and sworn antagonist of Lenin) took it for granted in 1904 that the respected theorist was thinking of a 'democratic' dictatorship of the proletariat.[4] For Kautsky, such a dictatorship was 'scarcely anything other than the unabetted rule of the class without compromise.'[5] In the end, therefore, the radical-sounding call for class dictatorship turns out to be little more than yet another call for proletarian isolation.

It should be pointed out that Kautsky's advocacy of working-class self-reliance was not without its ambiguities at certain points in time. In the mid 1890s, when he appears to have been at his most flexible, he wrote to the Austrian Social Democrat, Viktor Adler, of Bernstein and himself:

> We are probably the only two people in the party who talk about making compromises. It is desperately necessary at precisely this point in time. We are already powerful enough to influence the course of events, but not strong enough to be the dominant power. In this situation it's a waste of energy not to intervene in the internal struggles of the old parties and give them a direction which serves our interests.[6]

In fact Kautsky went so far as to characterise fear of compromise as a sign of immaturity. Significantly, however, these views were never published and Kautsky's position seems to have hardened in the course of the subsequent revisionist controversy.

Still in 1900 he discussed the possibility of entering a coalition government to defend working-class living standards; whilst his anti-Millerand resolution at the Paris Congress of the Second International in the same year was quite correctly described by one delegate as 'elastic', for it made a notorious distinction between questions of principle and questions of tactics. The participation of individual Socialists in bourgeois cabinets was condemned but, at the same time, the resolution envisaged situations in which Socialist parties could enter coalitions, albeit on a temporary basis. As Kautsky wrote: 'The question as to whether and to what extent the Socialist proletariat can participate in a bourgeois government is a question of tactics, which has to be answered differently at different times and in different places.'[7]

Twelve years later Kautsky had moved still further from a standpoint of total isolation, when he half-heartedly defended the SPD's decision to form an electoral pact with the Progressive Party. Such a policy he thought justified by the revitalisation of German Liberalism, which he attributed to the emergence of a 'new middle class' of white-collar workers. In 1912 Kautsky also insisted that there were issues on which the proletariat and sections of the bourgeoisie had common interests. We will see that this applied to the threat of war (as discussed in Kautsky's theory of 'ultra-imperialism') later.

Thus Kautsky's usual emphasis on working-class independence and self-reliance was not without its ambiguities before 1918. After that date, after the November Revolution and the erection of a parliamentary democracy in Germany, his position changed beyond recognition. This he admitted in 1920, though he also, and quite correctly, pointed out that the German political scene had also changed totally. Here we see something which will crop up again later: Kautsky's position before 1914 has to be related to the political institutions of the Second Reich. Originally he considered coalition government undesirable on the grounds that the semi-autocratic nature of the Empire would leave the socialists impotent and force them to identify with the utterly unacceptable policies of their coalition partners, policies which were anathema to both the principles of the party and the views of its supporters. After the Revolution and in a parliamentary state Kautsky believed that Social Democracy was strong enough to impose its views on its coalition partners. Furthermore, he became increasingly and understandably hyper-sensitive to the threat of counter-revolution, as embodied in the Free Corps and the emergence of radical right-wing movements such as Nazism. In this context Kautsky chided the Communists, who instituted a general and indiscriminate attack on everything that was not proletarian.

Kautsky's initial insistence on class-based politics stemmed from his economic analysis of exploitation in Capitalist society. It also rested upon a prognosis of the Capitalist future, identifying increasing class conflict, class polarisation and social revolution as its hallmarks. Again and again, even in the 1920s, Kautsky was to claim that as long as Capitalism existed, class conflict would become increasingly bitter, as a result of the laws of the Capitalist mode of production. One such central development was what Marx had described as *Verelendung* (the immiseration, or impoverishment of wage-labour). The theory of the increasing exploitation of the worker Kautsky defended against bourgeois critics, such as Max Weber and Tugan-Baranovsky, and against revisionists, such as Bernstein, who pointed to increasing working-class living standards. Kautsky's defence of the theory began by pointing out that the critics had simply failed to understand Marx. (In this respect I believe Kautsky to have been right. Apart from a crass remark which seems to claim absolute impoverishment in the *Manifesto,* the later writings, especially the second and third volumes of *Capital,* on occasion indicate a concept of immiseration far from absolute, recognising that trade-union

21

resistance can militate against wage cuts. This view is further borne out by Marx's scathing critique of Ferdinand Lassalle's 'iron law of wages' which did claim that wages were doomed to fall in absolute terms and that therefore strike action made no sense.) Kautsky accepted Bernstein's contention that working-class living standards had risen since the days of early Capitalism, but pointed out that this did not necessarily conflict with the theory of immiseration, for what this stated was that workers did not receive the full value of their labour, not that their wages were low in absolute terms. Trade-union struggle or state inter-vention could bring about improvements in wage levels and living standards but those improvements had to be seen in the context of higher productivity, engendered by the intensification of labour and technological modernisation, two processes which certainly took place in Imperial Germany before the First World War, as Dieter Groh's work has shown. These processes meant that the worker was receiving a lower percentage of the value of his labour-power than hitherto. Thus the rate of exploitation was increasing at the same time as wages were rising in absolute terms. Immiseration was thus a *relative* concept, denoting that profits were rising faster than wages and that labour's *share* of the national cake was declining. In fact Kautsky – again correctly – used official income tax statistics to demonstrate that higher incomes were rising more rapidly than lower incomes in the Second Reich, thus indicating a redistribution of wealth towards the wealthy. He also saw that it was the perception of this relative deprivation which was important, rather than the experience of low wages itself.

Increasing exploitation was one of the economic foundations upon which Kautsky erected his model of increasing class conflict. Another was the inevitability of economic crisis under Capitalism. Cyclical depressions were an integral and inevitable part of the Capitalist mode of production, not an unfortunate and avoidable by-product. Initially Kautsky's explanation of crisis was essentially underconsumptionist. As production was for exchange, for profit not use, so it was impossible for the individual Capitalist, producing in competition with his rivals, to judge demand. The 'anarchy of production' was a constant characteristic of Capitalist society. At the same time, the Capitalist was under constant pressure to increase production and productivity. Failure to produce at above the average rate of profit would lead to extinction at the hands of superior competition. The tendency of the rate of profit to fall as a result of increasing investment in ever more efficient and expensive machinery acted as a further spur to maximise the use of that machinery which could not be left to idle. So production rose by leaps and bounds. At the same time, demand could not expand without limitation. The central contradiction of wage-labour was that wages in Capitalist society served a double function. As an aspect of demand for the products of industry, the Capitalist had an interest in their increase. As a cost factor of production, on the other hand, the Capitalist had a vested interest in decreasing wages. Thus there was a limit beyond which wages could not rise without threatening profitability and as a result an ever greater quantity of goods was produced which had to find a market outside the working class. Since the Capitalists themselves were forced to plough back an increasing percentage of their returns into industry to remain competitive, they too were unable to absorb the surplus, nor could those sections of the community engaged in pre-Capitalist or agricultural forms of enterprise, for they were rapidly decreasing in number and provided insufficient aggregate purchasing power to absorb the increasing flood of production. Thus Capitalism both increased production and limited the size of its market. This was the root cause of the economic crises which dislocated production, forced prices down, threw workers onto the streets and showed that the Capitalist mode of production was not only exploitative but inefficient. Even colonial adventures, the conquest of new and distant markets by force, could not expand demand rapidly enough to cope with increased production. (See Chapter 4 on Imperialism).

In some of his later writings Kautsky rejected this underconsumptionist model of economic crisis. In opposition to Luxemburg's *Accumulation of Capital* (1913) and, for that matter in opposition to his own earlier theory, he declared in 1927 that Marx and Engels had never subscribed to such a model. With considerable justification from the later sections of *Capital* he now specifically rejected the notion that domestic consumption was necessarily incapable of absorbing increased production. The central problem lay in the disproportion between the production of producer goods and consumer goods, and between industry and agriculture. The agricultural sector was needed as a market for industrial goods and as a source of raw materials but that sector could not expand as rapidly as industry. Kautsky was already developing this theory before 1914, in which year he further claimed that the drive to overseas expansion on the part of the European powers was caused by the imbalance between their domestic industries and agriculture.

Whatever his explanation of Capitalist crisis, Kautsky remained sure that it was inevitable as long as private ownership of the means of production continued. Piecemeal reforms could not alter this situation. Such arguments came under increasing attack after the economic recovery of the late 1890s which to bourgeois economists, such as Max Weber, and to the Social Democrat Bernstein signalled that Capitalism had developed mechanisms to cope with imbalances between supply and demand. These critics argued that the development of trusts, cartels and new credit institutions, as well as accumulated experience, had enabled Capitalism to control production, limit competition and thus reduce the risk of crisis. Kautsky was not impressed by these arguments, which he believed to be generalisations from a short – and temporary – period of Capitalist recovery. Cartels and trusts could not ultimately obviate the 'anarchy of production'. Though they might lessen the impact of the economic crisis on the industrialist, they also brought new problems for the worker by increasing the power of capital over labour and depressing wages, even in periods of economic boom. Cartels were designed to maximise profits and keep prices high; they were not benevolent societies to protect the working class from insecurity. In short, an increasingly organised Capitalism entailed an increase in exploitation and conflict in which the trade unions found it increasingly difficult to defend their members' interests against powerful employers' associations. This gloomy prognosis was shared by Bebel and Luxemburg – hence her famous description of trade-union struggle as the 'labour of Sisyphus' – and was substantially correct for the decade before the outbreak of the First World War, when lock-outs enjoyed higher levels of success than strike action. Of course Kautsky's theories of Imperialism (see Chapter 4) also related to this debate. A central argument against the revisionists was that with increasing monopolisation of domestic production came a translation of Capitalist competition from the national to the international scene, bringing with it the threat of global conflict. As Capitalism developed, according to Kautsky, it continually augmented the productive powers of society and so increased the likelihood and intensity of economic crisis. Fortunately for its victims, however, a state of chronic overproduction indicated that the end of Capitalism was at hand and the abolition of private ownership of the means of production had become a necessity. This did not mean, however, that Capitalism would collapse 'automatically'. Over and over again Kautsky stressed that the creation of the Socialist society required *political action* on the part of the proletariat, of which more anon.

Karl Kautsky

Increasing exploitation and insecurity were thus the hallmarks of the proletarian future and central to Kautsky's belief that class conflict would increase in intensity. So also was a third, crucial tendency of Capitalist development: the concentration of capital and the polarisation of the classes. This process both created the seeds of the new society within the old – by increasing man's control over nature, by rationalising and increasing productive capacity and rendering the individual entrepreneur increasingly redundant in the face of ever more powerful corporate organisation – and increased social antagonism in the rotten fabric of the old. For Kautsky the Marxian theory of capital concentration was a vital question for socialism and Bernstein's critique thereof was the most important aspect of revisionist doctrine. It was of crucial importance because, if false, if the proletariat were not destined to increase in number, then a policy of working-class self-reliance made little sense and the chances of successful revolution were exceedingly thin. Consequently Kautsky invested a great deal of time and energy defending the thesis of class polarisation, which was the cornerstone of his _Social Revolution_ (1902), described by the German Chancellor von Bülow as the 'Red Baedeker', and of his _Road to Power_ (1909), a radical masterpiece predicting war and revolution which was much admired by Lenin. With the concentration of capital and the demise of the small concern came an inevitable increase in the size of the propertyless proletariat. The old handicraftsman and small producer was disappearing in the face of the superior competition of large-scale production, leaving capital and labour alone to fight the decisive battle of the class war.

There were several reasons for this development. Periodic crises forced down prices and ruined those small businesses with low profit margins and insufficient funds. The increasing deployment of ever more expensive machinery again required larger resources than the small producer could mobilise, thus increasing

26

the cycle of disadvantage. Kautsky was so convinced of the technical superiority of large-scale production, favoured by modern technology, that he confidently predicted the disappearance of the domestic craftsmen. When confronted by the statistics mobilised by his critics (in the 1907 census, for example, over a third of all those employed in 'industry and handicrafts' were either self-employed or worked in firms of five or fewer people) Kautsky retorted that many small firms were only nominally independent; they serviced the larger capital formations, which increasingly came to dominate. In any case, it was the massive concentrations of production in coal, iron, steel and chemicals which pointed to the future.

In the case of agriculture the situation was more problematic. Bernstein, Eduard David and many South German Social Democrats pointed out that peasant agriculture did not appear to be on the point of extinction. Indeed, David claimed that the number of peasant smallholdings was actually on the increase at the turn of the century and that this testified to the superiority of small-scale agricultural production, where family commitment and interest were more important than modern technology and supposed economies of scale. (Needless to say, this was again far more than an academic argument. What David and his colleagues wanted was to transform the SPD from a purely urban, industrial party into one that was also capable of mobilising peasant support.)

Kautsky deployed an armoury of arguments against those who advocated the adoption of a policy of peasant protection. He did modify his thesis of capital concentration in agriculture when confronted by evidence of the survival of small farms but he claimed that the survival of the peasant had been bought at considerable cost, both to the peasant and to the community at large. Some peasants had only survived by becoming outworkers in domestic industry, others had taken second jobs in the new factories. Thus the number of wage labourers was still increasing without the expropriation of the peasantry. Some new smallhold-ings were in fact the property of relatively affluent mine-workers and thus the proliferation of small farms grew *together* with the proletariat. Kautsky did concede that developments in agriculture were not identical to those in industry; there was a size of farm above which the advantages of scale disappeared; ground rent prevented investment in new technology and large-scale agricul-ture could only be successful where such technology, trained managers and skilled hands were available. The peasant had sur-vived but only at the expense of the consumer and agricultural progress. The peasant farm was incapable of providing the surplus essential for the creation of Socialism. From these somewhat disparate arguments Kautsky concluded that the SPD had no interest in policies of peasant protection.

Kautsky's refusal to embrace the peasantry as a worthy ally for the socialist movement and his scepticism concerning the survival of the 'old *Mittelstand*' of artisans, small shopkeepers and the like did not simply rest upon an analysis of their economic difficulties. If anything, it was even more dependent on arguments about the *politics* of these groups in an increasingly industrial society such as Germany. The continued existence of these 'left-overs' of an earlier mode of production did not diminish the severity of the struggle between Capital and Labour because these strata did not constitute 'classes' in any meaningful sense. This was because they were incapable of pursuing *independent* politics. They were both hostile to advancing Capitalism and yet clung to the ideal of private property. They were not bearers of a qualitatively different social order. Consequently the peasantry and the lower middle class vered wildly from course to course in their political allegiances. At times Kautsky considered these groups *as a whole* to be unreliable. On other occasions he identified internal divisions *within* these groups between the supporters of

Capital and the allies of Labour, divisions which he sometimes attributed to their differing clientèles. Yet as time went on, and not without justification, he became ever more convinced that the peasantry and the *Mittelstand* were increasingly conservative, that they defended existing property rights and that the Socialist movement would have to do battle with them. These groups were in fact becoming increasingly reactionary. They provided the rank and file of the anti-semitic movement, which gathered pace in the Germany of the 1890s. They had sold themselves to the forces of reaction for state protection, had allied themselves to the military, the bureaucracy and the landowners around the banner of Imperialism. 'Thus the petty bourgeoisie becomes more and more reactionary and unreliable' wrote Kautsky in 1907.[8]

The SPD's ideologue reproduced such arguments to combat the claims of Bernstein (and again Max Weber) that the class structure of advanced Capitalism was not becoming more polarised but increasingly differentiated and that the emergence of a 'new middle class' of white-collar salaried workers somehow mitigated class conflict. Kautsky was well aware of the emergence of this particular stratum and had commented on it at length, being impressed both by its absolute size and even more by the rate at which it was growing. None of this meant that the 'new middle class' constituted a 'class' in the fullest sense, however, It was far too heterogeneous in its social composition and divided in its political loyalties, proletarian in its economic position, but bourgeois in its social intercourse. Those members of this group who benefited indirectly from the production of surplus value – company directors, bank managers, opera singers (Kautsky's own motley crew!) – identified with capital in the class struggle. Yet as more and more people were educated, as office workers faced increasing competition for their jobs both from other human beings and from automation (in the guise of the female typist), so the vast majority of the 'new middle class' came closer to the proletariat in both their objective situation and their attitudes. Hence the appearance of this social stratum did not imply any reduction in the intensity of class conflict between capital and labour.

Again, however, the intensification of class conflict was no simple and mechanical consequence of economic developments and again, therefore, Kautsky's position was less mechanistic than that of many of his critics both within and outside the Social-Democratic camp. Equally important to Kautsky were the organisational and political moments of this process, the increasing *organisation* of social antagonists into classes. Obviously this was facilitated by the increase in size of the industrial working class and its concentration in larger units of production and in the working-class districts of industrial towns. It was also made easier by the increasing use of machinery which ironed out the differences between skilled and unskilled labour. Even the discipline of factory routine helped to breed discipline and solidarity in the Labour movement too. (Kautsky shared Lenin's distrust of 'unorganised' and 'spontaneous' protest, which was not the least reason for his controversy with Luxemburg.) However, the development of a revolutionary consciousness was *not* the inevitable outcome of struggles between capital and labour over wages and working conditions. Such struggles produced what Lenin subsequently described as 'trade-union consciousness' or 'economism' and this in turn explains why Kautsky was always somewhat scathing about the union movement which, he believed, should be placed firmly under the control of Labour's *political* wing.

This argument, of course, was perhaps Kautsky's most important contribution to Marxist theory: the theory of 'consciousness from without'. Significantly, when Lenin lifted it wholesale in *What is to be done?* (1902), it was Kautsky, not the Russian revolutionary tradition, which he quoted (with explicit acknowledgement). According to Kautsky, the proletariat required a coherent Socialist theory in order to be able to understand and to overthrow Capitalism. It was precisely the task of the *political party* to educate and organise its members into such a level of consciousness, for this could not come from trade-union struggle alone. It was the task of the party to inspire the working class with great aims, whereas the activities of the unions were restricted to the short-term and sectional gains of specific groups of workers. In 1901 Kautsky wrote in *Die Neue Zeit:* 'In any case science today is still a privilege of the property-owning classes. Thus the proletariat is incapable of creating on its own account a viable Socialist theory. Such a theory has to be brought to it.'[9] The worker could only gain a genuinely 'scientific' knowledge of Socialism with the aid of bourgeois intellectuals. Hence, concluded Kautsky: 'Socialist consciousness is therefore something carried into the class struggle of the proletariat from outside, not something that grows out of it automatically'.[10] Increasing class conflict thus resulted not only from the economic laws of motion of Capitalist society (capital concentration, crisis and exploitation), but also from the activities of the Socialist political party, from organisation and the induced revolutionary consciousness of the proletariat.

It was not only the proletariat which grew in strength and awareness as Capitalism developed. Kautsky noted that its enemy also became increasingly organised and politically aware. Indeed it was precisely this combined process which made the idea of a peaceful and effortless transition to Socialism illusory. The Capitalist had always had the press at his disposal, but now he could rely on other factors as well: initially the use of female, child and non-union labour, now the emergence of increasingly powerful employers' associations and the lock-out. Hence it was probable that the union movement might have to reckon with a serious setback in the near future and the Labour movement would have to develop new methods to combat exploitation.

The bourgeoisie was not only becoming stronger. In alliance with the landed elite, it was also beconing increasingly reactionary. The age of Liberalism was coming to an end as the German middle classes threw in their lot with the conservative military and bureaucratic establishment. Kautsky even detected similar developments in Britain after Chamberlain deserted to the Tories and espoused an Imperialist ideology. This theme of increasing reaction was taken up by all those within the SPD who believed, not without foundation, that Bernstein did not have a clue about the German situation. Bebel, Parvus, Karl Liebknecht, Luxemburg and Hilferding all echoed Kautsky's position when he wrote: 'Should parliamentary democracy develop in such a way as to threaten the rule of the bourgeoisie, then the bourgeoisie will prefer to repress such democratic forms of government, especially universal, direct and equal suffrage, rather than capitulate before the proletariat.'[11]

As in the case of Luxemburg and the younger Liebknecht, this issue was closely related to another, namely that of Imperialism. Kautsky's concern with Imperialism (see chapter 4) was not simply a concern with colonial expansion but also with the brutalisation of domestic politics in Europe and the emergence of new class alliances. In 1900, reflecting on the Boer War, he wrote: 'The more Manchester ideals are pushed into the background by Imperialism, and the more Imperialism becomes the basis of the political and social system, so social development becomes increasingly dependent on the force of arms and the more the power of Militarism grows.'[12]

In a sense, therefore, Kautsky's view of Imperialism was a response to the revisionist belief in an alliance with middle-class Liberalism, which, according to Kautsky, was doomed to failure. It is to the revisionist controversy and the critique of Kautsky's prognosis of class conflict and social revolution that we must now turn.

3   The revisionist controversy

In 1891, when it adopted the Erfurt Programme, the SPD had committed itself to the Marxist theory of class conflict, albeit in a vulgarised form. In the late 1890s, however, the premises of that theory, and of Kautsky's predictions, were increasingly called into question. The inevitability of economic crisis was denied, the thesis of immiseration declared invalid and the theories of capital concentration and class polarisation rejected. There was not going to be an 'inevitable' revolution and, as a result, Socialism was no simple matter of class interest, it was a matter of idealist conviction, a question of ethical choice. In the summary of Eduard Bernstein: 'Peasants do not shrink; middle class does not disappear; crises do not grow ever larger; misery and serfdom do not increase.'[13] Such ideas provided – and were intended to provide – the theoretical justification for the abandonment of Social Democracy's tactic of isolation and proletarian self-reliance. They were most clearly formulated in a series of articles entitled 'Problems of Socialism' which Bernstein wrote for *Die Neue Zeit* (Note that Kautsky authorised their publication) between 1896 and 1898 and most fully developed in the book *Die Voraussetzungen des Sozialismus* (normally known (in English) as *Evolutionary Socialism*) which appeared in the following year.

There had of course been other attacks upon the SPD's isolationist and class-based strategy long before Bernstein, initially an 'orthodox' Marxist, penned his 'revisionist' ideas. As early as 1879 the millionaire Karl Höchberg, at that time Bernstein's employer, and Carl Schramm, one of Kautsky's most bitter ideological antagonists, had advocated a more conciliatory attitude towards the German bourgeoisie and had regretted the party's commitment to the principle of class conflict. They wanted the SPD to abandon what they saw as its rigid ideological stance, to concentrate on 'practical' questions and to make some attempt to appeal to sections of the population other than indust-rial workers. Twelve years later, on 1 June 1891, in the Eldorado Palace in Munich, another attack was launched on the party's stance, this time by Georg von Vollmar, aristocrat and former radical, then leader of the Bavarian wing of the SPD. He claimed that the demise of the repressive measures of the Anti-Socialist Law in the previous year had transformed the face of German politics and that it was now both possible and necessary to adopt a strategy of reform within the existing order. A policy of total opposition to the Wilhelmine state had to be abandoned. (The speech caused such consternation among party ranks and gave rise to such hostility that Vollmar was henceforth less prepared to make public speeches on party policy, although he remained on the reformist side of the party.) As we have already seen, isolationist tactics were also called into question by Eduard David who advocated a 'positive' programme to win peasant votes.

None of this opposition quite shook the SPD's orthodoxy in the way that Bernstein was to do. Vollmar's speech was not concerned with the theoretical deficiencies of Marxism; he was more interested in immediate, practical issues. David only ques-tioned one aspect of Marxist theory. It was Bernstein who first provided a fully-blown theoretical justification for reformist tac-tics (collaboration with elements of the existing order), despite the fact that he started out with no such intention and repeatedly claimed that he was still a Marxist. In fact Bernstein himself admitted that 'systematic thought and logical progression sat heavily upon me',[14] a point picked up in turn by the defendants of Marxist orthodoxy, especially Rosa Luxemburg, who wrote indignantly and with Bernstein in mind that 'opportunism' was incapable of creating a 'positive theory' to match its practice.[15] In any case, what Bernstein began as a piece of 'good-natured social *bricolage'* (Nettl) did soon develop into a full-scale critique of the premises of Marxist argument. As we have already seen, for Bernstein Socialism was not a question of science but of ethics. Kautsky's attempts to identify 'laws' of Capitalist development were doomed, as man was not omniscient, and in any case intervention (not economic 'necessity') would bring about the Socialist order. Furthermore, central aspects of Marxist theory were found wanting. The theory of surplus value and the 'dialectic' (which Bernstein manifestly did not understand and regarded as a positivist statement concerning laws of social development) were incomprehensible mumbo-jumbo and could not be verified. The working class was not becoming more impoverished. The processes of capital concentration, cartelisation and monopolisation were succeeding at least partially in regularising Capitalist production. Thus economic crises were less likely and there would not be any final collapse, and thus Socialist revolution was not 'inevitable'. This point was reinforced by changes in the social structure of advanced industrial nations, where the emergence of a 'new middle class' would give rise to a more differentiated class structure and presaged a revitalisation of Liberalism. (In addition peasants and artisans were refusing to disappear, again contradicting a dichotomous model of society.) Above all Bernstein began to doubt that Capitalism would 'collapse'. (The fact that neither Marx nor Kautsky thought in such terms need not detain us here, Bernstein thought they did.) He wrote in the preface to *Evolutionary Socialism:* 'I set myself against the notion that we have to expect shortly a collapse of the bourgeois economy and that Social Democracy should be induced by the prospect of such an imminent, great social catastrophe to adapt its tactics to that assumption.'[16]

We have already seen Kautsky's response to these claims:

Bernstein had misconstrued the theories of immiseration and Capitalist crisis, had exaggerated the economy's stability and above all had failed to note that the bourgeoisie was becoming increasingly reactionary, not more prone to ally with labour. The ideas which Kautsky found so distasteful were not simply the product of the sceptical, but penetrating mind of a former bank clerk, of course. Revisionism was not spawned *ex nihilo* but was the fruit of the economic recovery which took place after 1896 (not only in Germany) and of a change in the political situation of the Second Reich. From 1896 until the First World War the German economy enjoyed almost uninterrupted growth and low levels of unemployment, even in the relatively bad years such as 1908-9. Between 1870 and 1913 weekly real earnings increased by thirty five per cent, with a really significant rise between 1880 and 1900 (though thereafter on acount of price inflation a period of stagnation, though not decline, set in). Increased earnings were reflected in increased living standards. Between 1892 and 1900 per capita meat consumption in Germany rose from 32.5 to 43.4 kilos. In 1896 at the start of the boom nearly seventy per cent of the population of Prussia had incomes below 900 Marks per annum. Only ten years later the figure was down to just over fifty five per cent. At the same time, those with incomes ranging from 900 to 3,000 Marks rose from twenty six per cent to 35 per cent of the taxpayers of that state. (Elsewhere I have argued that these figures are misleading for a variety of reasons. They do not reveal the still massive differentials between skilled and unskilled labour and between the different regions of the Reich – wages in the Ruhr, Saxony, Hamburg and Berlin tended to be much higher than elsewhere – and the even greater variation between male and female wages. The earnings curve of manual labour, which meant increasing difficulty and insecurity with illness and old age, and insecurity generated by seasonal unemployment are also masked by these figures. Compared to

Britain or the USA, Germany was still a relatively low wage economy in 1914. Higher wages were also brought at the cost of an increased pace of work and higher accident figures, especially in the mines. Yet it cannot be denied that there was a substantial improvement in working-class living standards in this period. Whether this makes labour less radical, as Bernstein imagined it would, is, however, a different question. This affluence actually witnessed an increase in SPD support, not a decline, whilst some of the most well-paid sections of the work force, such as miners and skilled metal workers, were also the most militant on both the industrial and the political front.)

If Bernstein's critique of revolutionary theory was fuelled by increased living standards, it was even further encouraged by relaxation on the part of the authorities. In 1890 the Anti-Socialist Law lapsed and although Social Democrats and trade-unionists were to be harassed in a variety of ways until 1914, at least the SPD enjoyed what might be described as a semi-legal existence. It could campaign openly and of course enjoyed a massive increase in its support. At the same time the 'New Course' of Chancellor Caprivi (1890-94) witnessed a willingness on the part of some sections of the German establishment to pursue more liberal economic policies, whilst the Imperial authorities instituted significant – though much overrated – reforms in the field of social welfare. The ideas of the distinguished academics, including the Webers, who formed the *Verein für Sozialpolitik* and who advocated the integration of Labour into the Imperial polity through welfare reform, were also conducive to a belief on the part of some (though never a majority within German Social Democracy) that class tensions might be on the decrease. Above all the SPD's electoral activities, the need to mobilise votes, including those of non-proletarian strata, provided a powerful impetus to those who wished to abandon the cherished (though in my opinion *not* self-imposed) strategy of isolation and raised the question of electoral alliance with parties of the middle class.

From these changed circumstances and certainly with an all too hasty optimism, Bernstein argued that the party should abandon its ivory tower and negotiate with the Liberals. 'I know of no principle', he wrote, 'which forbids all alliances, all compromises without exception'.[17] What the founding father of revisionism desired was the replacement of that section of the party programme declaring that the emancipation of the working class 'can only be the work of the proletariat' with a modified formula. It was precisely this that Kautsky and his friends found so unpalatable. Paul Fröhlich, leftist and biographer of Rosa Luxemburg, claimed in 1928 that the sole difference between the 'centrists' (Kautsky and his ilk) and the 'revisionists' was that the former did not wish to collaborate with sections of the bourgeoisie. The point has been repeated more recently, but was not lost on Kautsky's contemporaries either. Ignaz Auer, the party pragmatist and acute observer of the Social-Democratic scene, declared at the Dresden Congress of 1903 that the real point at issue was the revisionists' denial of class conflict and their consequent desire to establish links with the supposedly progressive sections of the bourgeoisie. Kautsky himself was quite explicit about the questions involved in his controversy with Bernstein and this issue in particular. He identified the concept of *limited* class conflict as central to revisionism and declared that his opponents wished to 'revise our relationship with specific sections of the bourgeoisie'.[18] He took exception to the idea that Socialist ideas were not class-specific, thought reconciliation between the classes an impossible dream and denied that democratic institutions rendered proletarian rule unnecessary. Bernstein and his supporters failed to see that organised labour must rely upon its own strength and that the class rule of the proletariat was still essential for its emancipation.

Thus Kautsky's controversy with Bernstein did have a practical significance and can only be understood 'in terms of practical concerns' (Nettl). It was not simply a question of words and related directly to the cornerstone of both Kautsky's political thinking and SPD strategy: a class-based isolationism. It was this immediate concern which led to the debate about Bernstein's ideas at the Hanover party conference of 1899 and at Dresden four years later. There are other senses, however, in which the debate did lack a tactical dimension. Much of the argument between Kautsky and his former (also later) friend took place at a high level of abstraction and with little explicit reference to tactics. In his classic defence of Marxist theory, *Bernstein und das Sozialdemokratische Programm* (1899), Kautsky was primarily concerned to defend the prognosis of Capitalist development and social revolution. He concentrated his energy and not inconsiderable talents on defending the theory of surplus value, economic crisis and class polarisation. In none of this did he suggest a specific tactic which would distinguish orthodox Marxists from revisionists or serve to root out the heresy. Also, as we shall soon see, both Kautsky and Bernstein remained Democratic Socialists.

This is not only true of Kautsky, however, but also other supposedly more radical defences of Marxism against Bernstein and his supporters. It is all too easy, for example, to draw an illusory distinction – in the light of subsequent developments – between Kautsky's position and that of Rosa Luxemburg at this point in time. A reading of the Polish revolutionary's *Sozialreform oder Revolution?* reveals how little she had broken away from her mentor. In that polemic Luxemburg stated that her major task was to defend the materialist conception of history and stress the *objective* necessity of Socialism. She wrote: 'In our opinion the crux of Bernstein's remarks is not to be found in his views about the practical tasks of Social Democracy but lies in what he has to say about the objective development of Capitalist

39

society, although those views [about tactics] are certainly connected with the latter'.[19]

Nettl's usually admiring biography of Luxemburg is compelled to admit that his subject's critique of Bernstein was highly abstract and primarily a defence of the SPD's long-established practice. It was not she who advocated specific measures to deal with the ideologically impure but Lenin who demanded their expulsion from the Social-Democratic camp, even if this meant splitting the party. Yet it was precisely this centralist line which Luxemburg could not stomach, as her critique of Bolshevik practice made amply clear in 1904, when she denounced such measures as 'artificial'. A dislike of autocratic leadership subsequently informed her caution concerning the affiliation of the Spartacus League (later the Communist Party – KPD) to the Third International, whilst the fact that the Spartacists only split from the SPD in 1917 in opposition to the Majority Socialists' support for the war effort, and even then remained in the hybrid Independent Social Democratic Party (USPD) until the end of December 1918, further testifies to her opposition to sectarianism.

In fact Luxemburg's critique of Bernstein stood firmly on the ground of the SPD's parliamentary strategy, much as she might despise 'parliamentary cretinism'. On close examination, the much vaunted insistence on the 'unity of theory and practice' turns out – at least at this point in time – to be an insistence on the unity of *reformist* practice with *revolutionary* theory. When, at the Stuttgart Congress of 1898, she claimed that the reformists had ceased to understand 'the relationship between our final goal and daily struggle' she admitted that the 'daily struggle' was at this stage a 'bourgeois' tactic. All she was saying was that a parliamentary practice could only serve the interests of the proletariat when inspired by the final aim of Socialism, by total opposition to bourgeois society. Hence it is hardly surprising that one delegate at Stuttgart complained that Luxemburg had promised to say something new, yet had ended her speech with nothing but commonplaces.

In a sense, therefore, Luxemburg's anti-revisionist polemic constituted precisely the same defence of theory in its own right as did that of Kautsky. Like him, she seriously believed that the whole strength of the modern Labour movement depended upon its theoretical grasp. It was theory alone which created the bond between the struggle for social reform, as a means to Socialism, and social revolution, the final aim. Even Parvus (Israel Helphand), who stood on the left of the party and was the first publicly to denounce Bernstein, took his position on the grounds of the SPD's parliamentary strategy, as in the famous article 'Opportunism in Practice' which appeared in *Die Neue Zeit* in 1901. His objection to the revisionist claim that 'the movement is everything to me, the end nothing' (a remark which Bernstein claimed was invariably misunderstood) was simply another vindication of a revolutionary goal *behind* reformist reality: he wrote of connecting the routine of parliamentary activity with the final goal of social revolution, not of a new tactic. It was to be some time before the left of the SPD found a tactical solution to revisionism and stagnation in the party in the mass strike and only then did the difference between Kautsky and Luxemburg become apparent.

Parvus and Hilferding said little during the revisionist controversy which Kautsky did not say and say at least as well, but they did take up arms against the threat of revisionism more quickly and with greater enthusiasm than their older colleague. In fact, it was Kautsky in his capacity as editor who had accepted Bernstein's 'Problems of Socialism' for publication in *Die Neue Zeit* and who initially turned down polemics against his friend on the grounds that they rested on a 'mistaken' view of Bernstein's intentions. It was not the SPD's official theorist who led the challenge to the new heresy but Parvus, writing in his own *Sächsische Arbeiterzeitung* between 28 January and 6 March 1898.

Kautsky was still slow to act and Rosa Luxemburg's critiques of revisionism (subsequently to apper as 'Social Reform or Revolution?') in the radical *Leipziger Volkszeitung* in the September of that year also beat him to the draw.

Kautsky's hesitation in such a serious matter is virtually an unwritten episode in his intellectual development and important in two respects. It reveals a personality ridden by more doubts than his printed works suggest. George Lichtheim's description of the Social Democrat as 'one of those fortunate people who never encounter a serious doubt or feel uncertain about the direction of their interests' is definitely wide of the mark in this respect.[20] The episode is also instructive, in so far as it reveals what Kautsky ultimately held most dear in Marxist theory.

This uncharacteristic hesitation (contrast it to his reaction to the Bolshevik revolution almost twenty years later) puzzled many of his colleagues and, in particular, the Russian Marxists who had often looked to him for guidance. Martov mused: 'Who would have thought that the bloodthirsty "Montagne" of our days possessed such a store of good nature',[21] whilst Plekhanov was especially upset. Asking what remained of Marxism if Bernstein were right, Plekhanov declared: 'In all truth we would be forced to reply "not much": or rather "nothing at all"' (letter of 20 May 1898). He demanded to know why Kautsky had made no public response and was quite adamant: 'Bernstein must be annihilated' (letter of 16 September 1898). August Bebel, the aged and distinguished leader of the SPD but by no means its most clear-headed theoretician, was also perplexed by Kautsky's silence. He wrote to his party comrade: 'What would Engels say if he could see how Eddie is undermining everything that he himself has helped to build.' (Letter of 15 February 1898.) Later, after Kautsky had begun to take up the challenge, Bebel still wanted to know why he had made so many 'concessions' to the revisionists (letter of 9 September 1899).

In part Kautsky's hesitancy can be explained by personal loyalty. No-one was ever closer to him than the man he had first met in Zürich and with whose help he had first begun to propagate the gospel of Marxism during the Anti-Socialist Law. His personal correspondence reveals what a trauma it was to break with Bernstein. (Plekhanov does seem to have been aware of this, despite his strictures.) It must have been hard for Kautsky to accept that one who had done so much for the spread of Marxism in Germany, one who had been so instrumental in his own conversion to the doctrine and whom Engels had entrusted with Marx's legacy, could turn away from his former mentors so easily. Bebel testifies that Kautsky had long been arguing with Bernstein in private correspondence: 'Always with hope of saving him for Marxism' (Bebel to Adler 4 Novembert 1898). That same hope Kautsky revealed in another letter, also to Viktor Adler: 'I would not like you to misunderstand my view of Eddie. Of a fall from grace, in the sense of going over to the enemy, there is no question. But Eddie has become uncommonly sceptical, more sceptical than his articles suggest' (letter of 9 April 1898).

As already indicated, Bernstein did not set out to mount a full-scale attack on Marxist theory, merely to raise some questions about recent social development. Hence it is understandable that Kautsky's opposition was slow to form. What is surprising is his initial enthusiasm for Bernstein's work, to which he was 'most sympathetic'[22] and which he regarded as a continuation of something he and Engels had begun a few years earlier, namely an attempt to comprehend recent economic developments. Hence at the Stuttgart Conference, although making it clear that he disagreed with his friend's ideas, Kautsky insisted that the party should be grateful for such stimulus. It was this tolerance which so enraged Plekhanov (also in attendance).

In correspondence with Bernstein, Kautsky accepted some criticism of the labour theory of value, claimed that the principal difference between them was 'optimism and pessimism' in evaluating the same situation and even took a tolerant line on the dictum that 'the movement is everything'. What Kautsky was not sure about, however, was where Bernstein's ideas were leading and what Bernstein intended to put in the place of the theories he criticised. On 10 June 1898 Kautsky wrote: 'You would disappoint us greatly, should you leave off at the pro-legomena, at what is wrong with the old doctrine. You have thrown our strategy overboard, our theory of value, our philosophy. Everything now depends on what new things you intend to replace the old'.[23]

Clearly Kautsky approached Bernstein's writings in the late 1890s in a mood that was far from doctrinaire. Yet one can exaggerate his receptiveness to the new ideas. When he finally realised exactly where Bernstein was going, then tolerance changed to hostility. This was how Kautsky portrayed his own painful development through the revisionist controversy much later, but it was already implicit in a letter to Bernstein of 30 August 1897, in which he refused to abandon either the materialist conception of history or the idea that the proletariat would be the driving force of the coming revolution: 'Should once the materialist conception of history and the concept of the proletariat as the driving force of the coming social revolution be eclipsed, then I would have to confess that I would be finished, then my life would have no meaning'.[24]

As we have seen, Kautsky did ultimately write against revisionism in an impressive work of 1899: *Bernstein and the Social-Democratic Programme. An Anti-Critique.* Although not advocating any new strategy, he defended the SPD's isolationist and class-based stance. He would not relinquish his belief that class conflict was increasing in intensity and would continue to do so. He steadfastly maintained that both capital and labour were growing in strength and becoming conscious of their antagonistic interests.

A policy of reaction might be anticipated to defend the existing order against the threat constituted by the organised Labour movement. Such a policy was also associated with another aspect of advanced capitalism: Imperialism.

4   *Imperialism*

N. N. Roy, founder member of the Indian Communist Party, spoke in ignorance when he claimed that the Second International had 'failed to appreciate the importance of the colonial question. For them the world did not exist outside Europe'.[25] Peter Nettl was equally mistaken in his claim that Kautsky 'notably failed to appear among those who contributed to a special theory of Imperialism'.[26] In fact Kautsky was, to my knowledge, the first Marxist to develop a fully coherent theory of economic Imperialism, as Hugo Haase pointed out to Kautsky's critics at the founding conference of the USPD at Gotha in 1917. What is more, Kautsky's claim to precedence rests not on his well-known 'Theories of Crises' articles in *Die Neue Zeit* in 1901-2, which appeared just before J. A. Hobson's famous work on *Imperialism* (1902), but on articles written as early as 1884 in the same journal (which again preceded the earlier writings of Hobson on the subject).

Kautsky first employed the term 'Imperialism' in a quite specific sense in 1900, when writing about the decline of laissez-faire Manchester ideas in Britain and about the Boer War. Throughout his long career he more usually spoke of 'Colonialism' *(Kolonialpolitik),* but his interest in the phenomenon of colonial expansion and its *domestic* (n.b.) consequences had beeen aroused long before the turn of the century. He himself claimed to have been the first Socialist to take the matter seriously and by 1902 he saw European expansion overseas as the decisive characteristic of his age, as the hallmark of a 'new period'.[27] At first, Kautsky's interest in colonial expansion had been dominated by a human sympathy for its exploited and helpless victims. In 1883 he insisted that colonial enterprises were exploitative ventures and questioned the fashionable, if transparent, doctrine that Germany (and other European nations) had a 'civilising' mission amongst the backward and superstitious natives. This primarily ethical objection to Colonialism remained with Kautsky for the rest of his life and was constantly evident in all his writings on the subject. He decried the expropriation of North American Indians and criticised the plantation system in Australia. At the Stuttgart conference of the Second International he rejected the suggestions of the Dutchman Van Kol and, interestingly, of Bernstein that Europe's task was to civilise the non-European world, claiming that 'Colonialism is opposed to the politics of civilisation',[28] a point made by Wilhelm Liebknecht earlier, but not shared by several within pre-war German Social Democracy, such as Max Schippel, Joseph Bloch and Gustav Noske. Kautsky, on the other hand, argued that colonial expansion invariably entailed the forcible expropriation of the native inhabitants and 'plunder'.[29]

It was in 1884, at a time when for most Social Democrats 'Imperialism' was associated with the personal rule of the Kaiser and the Prussian military rather than the dynamics of Capitalist production, that Kautsky first attempted to explain the rash of overseas expansion on the part of the major European powers in structural terms, in terms of the laws of Capitalist development. The attempt was not wholly original, of course. Many Conservative and Liberal advocates of Imperial expansion stressed its economic necessity. Jules Ferry, the French politician, spoke of his government's colonial policy as 'the child of our industrial policy' and believed overseas markets essential to prevent domestic revolution. Even Bismarck, whose colonial policies of the 1880s have more often been explained in terms of international diplomacy or domestic politics, gave similar reasons for German overseas expansion. The core of the economic model of

Imperialism – an underconsumption theory – had already been present in the work of Sismondi, Wakefield and Robert Owen, the last of whom linked it to working-class impoverishment. More significantly for Kautsky, Marx somewhat ambiguously and Engels more decisively had rooted underconsumption in the laws of Capitalist production and had seen overseas markets as one possible response to the problem. But what they did not do, as Kautsky by contrast did, was to link an underconsumption theory to the forcible annexation of overseas territories. Such annexation had been seen by Marx and Engels, at least in the case of India, rather as a means of primary and pre-capitalist ('primitive') accumulation.

Writing anonymously in *Die Neue Zeit* in 1884, Kautsky produced a theory of Capitalist overproduction which necessitated the export of surplus goods to the undeveloped regions of the globe. In this model, commodity production yielded a surplus that neither the worker nor the Capitalist could consume, for the reasons set out earlier. Nor could those sections of the population engaged in precapitalist sectors of the economy consume this surplus for these were necessarily contracting under the impact of industrialisation. Foreign markets *within* Europe were unable to absorb the surplus because of the customs barriers and tariffs which had been erected in the wake of the economic depression of the 1870s. (Germany had instituted major tariffs in 1879.) Consequently, colonial territories were important for the industrial nations as a market for surplus production. They had become essential for the survival of Capitalism. Already, however, Kautsky recognised that there was a limit to what these colonial markets could purchase and at this early stage reckoned that independence movements in the colonies threatened the whole system with collapse.

Such was the first theory of Economic Imperialism, which Kautsky repeated two years later. Capitalism could only survive if its markets were expanded continually. As a consequence: 'The Capitalist class is today searching feverishly for new markets to get rid of its over-production'.[30] Again, however, such expansion had its limits; new markers were not being opened up as quickly as production increased, a point reiterated by Kautsky in 1891.

Between that day and 1898, however, Kautsky made several significant modifications to this theory. He continued to see the export of surplus goods as one of the driving forces of colonialism but, like the Italian socialist Turati and even more famously Joseph Schumpeter, he now began to argue that its main beneficiaries were the parasites of the Capitalist state, rather than industrial capital itself. He wrote:

> And if one looks more closely, one also finds that it was not the needs of industrial development which brought about the latest phase of colonialism, but on the one hand the needs of classes whose interests stand opposed to the needs of economic development and on the other the needs of a particular type of state, whose interests stand opposed to those of advanced civilisation. In other words, just like protectionist policies, the most modern phase of Colonialism is the work of *reaction*. [31]

Imperial expansion was now related to the atavistic mentality and interests of the pre-industrial elite, in particular of the military, bureaucracy and high finance.

Financial capital was seen as playing an especially important role in the formation of colonial policy, though whether financial capital was an advanced or a backward fraction is unclear. The accumulation of a large quantity of capital at a time when the rate of profit was falling in the advanced industrial states stimulated the search for more lucrative investments overseas, where government indebtedness and a more labour-intensive economy guaranteed higher returns on investment. The returns on that investment could only be secured, however, where it was protected by the state; and as states were more prepared to engage in overseas conquests to divert attention from class conflict at home, so the era of colonial expansion had arrived. An analysis of the Boer War in 1900 strengthened this line of argument. For, according to Kautsky, that war only served the interests of a small clique. With the end of the era of free trade in the depression of the 1870s and the advent of more severe competition from other industrialising states, the English Capitalist had to turn to the state for help – an unprecedented step in the classic land of Manchester ideals – to ensure a large protected market by the acquisition of overseas colonies. At first this appeal had met with a good deal of opposition as the military and bureaucratic interests were less fully developed in Britain than in Germany. But high finance, which had the greatest interest in and the most to gain from Colonialism, and the interest of heavy industry had won the day. (In this struggle these forces had even been aided by sections of the English working class, which also had something to gain from the exploitation of underdeveloped regions and which felt themselves in something of a privileged position vis-à-vis the rest of the world.) Kautsky had now come to the conclusion that capital, especially commercial and financial capital, needed an ever expanding sphere of influence and power to prosper and that it was the military, bureaucracy and high finance who benefited from colonial adventures. He wrote: 'The policy of colonial expansion is less a struggle to annex new markets than a struggle to conquer new fields of activity for the military, bureaucracy and high finance.'[32] In the following year, in 1901, Kautsky somewhat uneasily combined his earlier underconsumptionist model with his later insistence on the role of financial capital. European countries still needed to export surplus consumer goods, but they were also now exporting producer goods and the capital to buy these. The territorial expansion of the industrial states was now related directly to their domestic processes of capital concentration. The development of cartels, trusts and monopolies was one strategy to cope with overproduction and just as important as the related drive to acquire protected overseas markets. At the same time, those industries which were most concentrated were precisely those which pressed most strongly for the introduction of protective tariffs and colonial expansion, so as to monopolise an ever greater 'domestic' market.

Kautsky's discussion of Imperialism in the 'Theories of Crises' articles of 1902 seemed to lay more stress on Capitalist overproduction again, stressing that the new markets, which still could never expand rapidly enough, were necessary to absorb surplus products. Yet this reversion signified no real change of mind, but was rather a function of the fact that those articles were primarily intended to defend the Marxist theory of inevitable economic crisis aginst the Russian economist Tugan-Baranovsky, who argued that domestic markets might well be sufficient to enable a permanent reproduction of the Capitalist system. In fact it was not until 1907, in *Socialism and Colonialism,* a work of some influence and considered by Bebel to be the best thing Kautsky had ever written, that the editor of *Die Neue Zeit* returned to the significance of financial capital in overseas expansion. Although less impressive than Rudolf Hilferding's momunental *Financial Capital* which appeared three years later, *Socialism and Colonialism* did succeed in drawing together the processes of depression, capital concentration, monopolisation, overproduction and colonial expansion. (I suppose the problem of the work is precisely that it is such a *pot pourri,* tries to have it too many ways at once). The unavoidable overproduction/underconsumption of the Capitalist system led to economic crisis. In order to cope with this, the Capitalists tried temporarily to lower labour productivity, to increase wastage by promoting armaments sales and to limit competition by a process of monopolisation, thereby main-

taining profits without increasing production. Capital was
exported, mainly to agrarian regions which were annexed by the
colonial power to make returns on investment there more secure.
For Capitalism to survive, Colonialism had become an economic
necessity.

This theory of Imperialism was soon abandoned by Kautsky.
Between 1911 and 1914 he resuscitated one aspect of his first
theory (the primacy of *industrial* capital's needs to export and
need for raw materials) but now deployed it in quite a different
fashion. The desire of Capitalist states to annex agrarian regions
was now explained in terms of the relationship between domestic
industry and agriculture. The former expanded much more
rapidly than the latter, which it needed as a market and a source
of raw materials. This created an imbalance between the two
sectors which led to an economic crisis in which producer and
consumer goods could no longer be exchanged. The dilemma
explained the desire of industrial capital to expand the agricultural
territory at its disposal and Imperial expansion was *one* particular
way of doing this. Significantly, financial capital played only a
secondary role; the export of capital served to further the ends
of industrial capital, by developing communications and technical
improvements in agriculture. Capital could just as easily have
been used to develop industry, as in the USA and Tsarist Russia.

It was this, Kautsky's last theory of Imperialism, to which
Lenin, previously an admirer, took such violent objection. The
nature of that objection, however, had less to do with their
dispute over the causes of Imperialism (Lenin stressed the *primacy*
of financial capital in the process, which he did not simply reduce
to overseas colonisation but also capital penetration of Russia)
than with the relationship between Imperialism, war and revolution. In his earlier theories and especially in *The Road to Power*
(1909) Kautsky had always maintained that the quest for colonies
created conflict between the great powers and that the sub-

sequent arms race brought with it the danger of war. Indeed, even after the First World War he maintained that the arms race and, to a certain extent, Imperial ambitions had been responsible for the catastrophe which took millions of working men to their graves. Where Kautsky changed his mind, however, was on the question of the inevitability of war in the Imperialist stage of Capitalism. He came to question Lenin's view that Imperialism was the 'final stage of Capitalism'. This had not been so earlier, when Kautsky was much in agreement with his party leader Bebel, who declared: 'Wars are therefore of the essence of Capitalism. They will not cease until the Capitalist order has been outlived'.[33] In 1899 the editor of *Die Neue Zeit* declared wars to be unavoidable in capitalist society, going on to predict two years later that, when all the regions of the globe had been annexed by the industrial powers: 'Then there will be only *one single* way left to extend the area of monopoly further: no longer conflict between industrial state and agrarian state, but the bloody conflict of the great industrial states with one another: world war'.[34] Writing in 1907 he again saw Militarism as a consequence of Capitalism and war, if it came, as a consequence of Imperialism and the arms race.

By 1912 Kautsky's position had changed beyond recognition. The earlier pessimism had been replaced by a cautious optimism. Although in no doubt that the arms race was a consequence of Imperialism and economic necessity, Kautsky now refused to admit that the present *form* of Imperialism was a necessary and final stage of Capitalism. Imperialism was certainly not fortuitous but neither was it necessarily synonymous with Capitalism's still admittedly necessary attempts to conquer new markets. The present way of violence was merely one particular way of doing this. The arms race was no longer indispensable to Capitalist development and Imperialism was not a 'magic formula' which explained all that was happening in the contemporary world.[35]

The SPD's theorist continued to believe that the subjugation of
the colonial people could only be ended by native insurgency or
proletarian revolution in the industrial state itself but this did
not mean that the present form of Imperialism was either the
last stage of Capitalism or even an inevitable stage. As a rule
colonies were bad business and unnecessary for industrial
advance; a point which made considerable sense to the German
taxpayer, for only two of the Second Reich's colonies (Togoland
and Samoa) were financially self-supporting. In fact American
Capitalism had done so well precisely because it had avoided
wasteful expenditure on colonial enterprises. On this specific
point Kautsky was able to employ a stock of arguments long
familiar not only to Social Democracy but even to the small
Liberal opposition in Wilhelmine Germany. The cost of Imperial
adventures, and especially of military expenditure, had long been
in the forefront of SPD criticism, and with good reason: by 1913
the deficit on colonial budgets had cost the Reich (and therefore
the taxpayer) over one thousand million marks. It is scarcely
surprising that Georg von Vollmar demanded that the 'burden'
be lifted[36] and that Bebel saw Colonialism as benefitting only a
small clique of very particular interests.

Kautsky went even further than this in his later writings. By
generating friction between the powers and creating the arms
race, colonial expansion had entailed a vast wastage of valuable
resources. It made further economic development more difficult,
not easier, and brought the threat of war. War itself constituted
the greatest danger to the Capitalist economny. Capitalism, whose
interests were best served by improving communications and a
policy of free trade, needed peace to develop. Thus it was 'not
the furtherance but the abolition of militarism' which was the
essential prerequisite for economic progress.[37] Under these
circumstances Kautsky believed that it was not impossible for
the Capitalist nations to recognise an interest in a peaceful resol-

ution of their conflicts through a process of international cartelisation, a process described by Kautsky as 'Ultra-Imperialism'. He wrote: 'From a purely economic point of view it is therefore not out of the question that Capitalism will enter a new phase: the translation of cartelisation onto an international plane, a phase of Ultra-imperialism. This phase we will of course have to combat just as energetically as Imperialism; but its dangers lie in quite a different direction, not in the arms race and a threat to peace'.[38] This volte-face on Kautsky's part seems to have had several distinct origins. Around 1911 there seemed to be a distinct change in the diplomatic climate. The agreement of Great Britain and Russia on the demarcation of spheres of influence in Persia, Afghanistan and Tibet, the solution of the Samoan crisis, Franco-German compromises on Morocco, Anglo-German agreements on the future of the Portuguese colonies and simply the fact that several international crises had *not* led to war bred a certain optimism, as did the London conference after the Second Balkan Crisis. Kautsky was not alone in his response to these developments. Indeed, as Georges Haupt pointed out, one of the reasons why much of the Marxist left was so unprepared for the outbreak of war in the summer of 1914 was precisely because the theory of 'Ultra-imperialism' and peaceful development had become so widely held within the Second International. Hermann Molkenbuhr, a prominent member of the SPD and one of the paid secretaries of the International, saw little danger in the Agadir crisis because French and German firms were co-operating in the exploitation of Morocco. As a result, he believed that war 'could injure the interests of the greatest Capitalists, who have a sharp eye for their interests and will call a halt in time'.[39] Even Bebel, who had for long reflected gloomily on the danger, even the inevitability, of catastrophe now looked forward to a 'completely new era of international Colonialism'.[40]

Perhaps the most important aspect of Kautsky's change of

mind, however, was his intense horror of war and his desire to prevent it, even in a situation in which revolution seemed distant. This involved the German Social Democrat in a not inconsiderable dilemma, as Paul Lensch and Karl Radek pointed out in a heated polemic in 1912. For if Imperialism and war were the necessary consequences of the Capitalist mode of production, as Kautsky had once seemed to believe, then demands for disarmament and a League of Nations *before* the social revolution made no sense. Significantly it was in the course of his debate with Lensch that Kautsky first began to approach his theory of Ultra-imperialism, denying that Militarism was a necessary adjunct of Imperialism and arguing that it was possible to do something about it immediately. In clear breach of much of his earlier thinking he now claimed that sections of the bourgeoisie could be mobilised against military expansion, for *industrial* capital was not necessarily warlike and had an interest in the preservation of peace. (This explains further why Kautsky's later theory of Imperialism tended to play down the role of financial capital, which he did believe to be imbued with a militaristic spirit. In this respect, in ignoring the dominance of financial capital, Kautsky clearly found himself at odds with Lenin and, for that matter, Hilferding.) In fact Lenin, Lensch and others were right in maintaining that the theory of Ultra-imperialism and Kautsky's repeated appeals for disarmament bore a strong resemblance to revisionist arguments on domestic politics; for Kautsky was now saying that, in alliance with progressive sections of the bourgeoisie, the arms race and war could be prevented *within* the framework of Capitalist society. This was why Lenin dismissed the theory as a 'stupid little fable',[41] one which postponed the date of Capitalism's collapse and of the revolution. For Lenin, revolution and only revolution, not peace treaties and disarmament, was the way to end war and, in turn, war brought the possibility of successful revolution, indicating that Capitalism was in its death throes.

This Kautsky denied. He had once argued that wars could destroy obsolete social and political formations. He had argued in the past that wars meant unavoidable revolution, though he was never totally clear on this point. Though at times he suggested that wars might create a revolutionary climate by weakening the ruling authorities, generating discontent amongst the masses and swelling the revolutionary ranks, he also noted that those very factors which generated such a situation were also the very opposite of what he saw as the prerequisites of Socialist construction (giant productive forces and peace). Even in his radical masterpiece *The Road to Power* (1909) Kautsky claimed that a proletariat which came to power as a result of war might well prove incapable of realising Socialism, for war was the 'most irrational means' of revolutionary change.[42]

All these considerations presented Kautsky with very real problems on the actual outbreak of war in August 1914 for which he was – like so many of his colleagues – utterly unprepared. For the 'social-chauvinists' within German Social Democracy it was Germany's mission as the most advanced Capitalist nation with the most advanced proletariat to conquer. (Interestingly the former leftists Lensch and Haenisch, who had previously stated the inevitability of war under Capitalism and the futility of disarmament, now found themselves equating German victory with social revolution.) Many of the revisionists and reformists within the party believed that the war offered an opportunity to break the mould of Imperial politics; in return for support for the war effort the government would be forced to grant to the trade unions and to the SPD an unprecedented degree of political recognition. In fact the whole political structure would have to change. For party and trade-union functionaries a prime concern was the preservation of their massive organisational empires, whilst for many party members the most relevant consideration was the genuinely held belief that Germany was about to embark

57

on a *defensive* war and, even more significantly, a war of defence against autocratic Russia. This position was certainly not restricted to the right of the party and was to a certain extent shared initially by many, such as Kautsky himself and Kurt Eisner, who subsequently came to decry the SPD's support for the nation's war effort. Only a small group of the extreme left of the party denounced the war from the start as an Imperialist venture and even they took some time to come round to Lenin's position of 'revolutionary defeatism'. (It is not without interest that the most prominent anti-war campaigner in German Social Democracy both before and during the war, Karl Liebknecht, was in fact extremely confused in his theoretical position. In his *Anti-Militarism* (1907), for example, one will find *both* the advocacy of disarmament, international peace-keeping institutions etc. *and* the claim that wars are inevitable as long as Capitalism survives.) Kautsky's position differed from most of the above. Kautsky denied that the war could simply be explained by colonial rivalries, believed – along with Lenin as well as most Social Democrats – that the idea of preventing war through a general strike was illusory and claimed that peace was essential for the triumph of proletarian revolution (this time a most un-Leninist position). From 1915 onwards, recognising that the German war effort was not exclusively defensive, Kautsky called repeatedly for 'peace without annexations', as in *The Demand of the Hour* (1915) which he wrote with Hugo Haase and Kurt Eisner. This position ultimately brought him into conflict with the leadership of the SPD, led to his dismissal from the editorship of *Die Neue Zeit* in 1917 and pushed him into the ranks of the Independent Social Democratic Party founded at Gotha in the same year.

On the issue of Imperialism, therefore, Kautsky produced many, often contradictory, theories. His final belief in the possibility of a peaceful form of Imperialsim (achieved in conjunction with progressive elements of the bourgeoisie) clearly deviated from the earlier and more isolationist pessimism. His initial stance, however, which predicted increased international tension, the arms race and the probability of war on the international scene was also, as we have seen already, intended to match the prognosis of increasing domestic class conflict. The brutalisation and increasingly reactionary nature of the European bourgeoisie was in Kautsky's mind also linked to aggressive extra-European expansion and new class alliances, in which the middle class, and especially the German middle class, became even less liberal and all the more inclined to embrace the old landed elite and the backward-looking *Mittelstand* in anti-labour groupings. This was part of the response to revisionist and reformist illusions of gradual and peaceful progress. It also raised a question. If reaction were to be the order of the day, how should the SPD respond? It was in this context that there emerged a second serious challenge to Kautsky's orthodoxy, this time from the left.

5   *The mass strike*

The theory of Imperialism was initially a source of support for that thesis of increasing class conflict which Kautsky sought to defend against Bernstein. The unity of the forces of reaction around the Imperialist banner threatened the prospect of repression. The German bourgeoisie was forsaking constitutionalism and possessed be threatened and especially if there was an attempt was the SPD to do, should what limited constitutional rights it possessed be threatened amd especially if there was an attempt to end universal suffrage for the Reichstag, from which Social Democracy so manifestly benefited?

Kautsky had no doubt that his party must defend those rights and institutions with extra-parliamentary means if necessary. As early as 1893 he had looked to the mass strike (so called to demarcate it from the anarchist conception of a 'general strike') in this context and he in fact claimed that he was the first Socialist to propagate the idea. In that year he called for the SPD to debate the mass strike, which he believed would play an increasingly important role in the future, but met with little response. It was really in the wake of the failure of the second Belgian general stike in 1902 that the issue became more real, as Rosa Luxemburg blamed the leaders of Belgian Socialism, not for calling the strike but for the half-hearted way it had been pursued. She already saw that such a weapon might serve to augment the parliamentary strength of the Labour movement (though significantly not to *replace* it). By the following year the prospect of a mass strike in Germany had become an issue, as Rudolph Hilferding believed that a reactionary coup might seek to overthrow universal suffrage to the Reichstag and that therefore the use of the mass strike as a defensive weapon could become necessary. Such enthusiasm for the new tactic was not shared by the right of the SPD, nor – more significantly – by the leadership of Germany's Socialist-affiliated Free Trade Unions. Gustav Eckstein, amongst others, calculated that such a tactic might lead to ignominious defeat and the destruction of the trade-union movement and all it had achieved. This was to remain the essential position of the Free Trade Unions throughout the mass-strike debate; the concrete gains of piecemeal, routine trade-union work should not be put at risk by political adventures.

This position was not that of the so-called localist unions, which had opposed trade-union centralisation and bureaucratisation from the early 1890s and which, although numerically small, had some influence amongst miners in the Ruhr and metal and building workers in Berlin. These organisations had moved in an 'anarchosocialist' direction and in 1904, led by Dr Rafael Friedeberg, they took up the issue of the mass strike, but in a way that was quite different to Hilferding and Kautsky. For Friedeberg the mass strike was not simply a supplement to the Labour movement's parliamentary strategy but was rather an *alternative,* for parliamentary tactics threatened the SPD with stagnation, corruption and an increasingly 'bourgeois' view of the world. Such ideas were even more anathema to the trade-union leadership, of course, than those of Hilferding. Thus Robert Schmidt, trade-union leader and Social-Democratic parliamentary deputy, declared at the 1904 Congress of the Second International in Amsterdam: The general strike would do more harm to the proletariat and its organisation than even the actual class situation'.[43] Ignaz Auer, a leading pragmatist in the SPD, was even more dismissive: 'The general strike is general nonsense'.

The whole issue of the mass strike really came alive in the following year, however, a year which witnessed revolution, albeit abortive, and mass strikes in Russia, and widespread labour unrest in Germany itself, involving over half a million workers. In this context Kautsky and several other leading Social Democrats pressured the party leadership to debate the tactic. Kautsky wrote a preface to Henriette Roland-Holst's *General Strike and Social Democracy* (1905), defending that work against an irate party executive, and fulminated against the SPD's central organ *Vorwärts* for trying to prevent discussion of the mass-strike tactic. He argued that it was the strongest weapon available to the working class and was assuming an even greater importance as it became political in motivation. The political strike was the 'purest'[44] weapon of the class war and might well play the role that barricades had played in the revolutions of the past. Above all, it was the weapon to be used to counter a reactionary coup aimed at destroying universal suffrage.

Such was the radical appearance of Kautsky's interventions in the mass-strike debate of 1905. However that appearance was extremely misleading, as his subsequent and notorious controversy with Rosa Luxemburg was to reveal. Kautsky certainly defended the right of the party left to *discuss* the mass-strike tactic. He was also quite prepared to contemplate its use *in abstract*. What he never did, however, was advocate its use in any concrete situation. In his polemical writings against anarchists and Utopian Socialists Kautsky had always placed great emphasis on the more deterministic aspects of Marxian thought. In his debate with Bernstein he had stressed the objective developments which made social revolution not only possible but virtually unavoidable. Now, when discussing the mass strike, Kautsky fell victim to that determinism and argued the following unpleasant truths to his less patient and more adventurous colleagues. Although any political organisation had to fight hard to survive, it could not launch itself into mass actions regardless of the consequences. Furthermore, argued Kautsky, there were a host of prerequisites which had to be met before a mass strike could even be contemplated. This exhaustive list of conditions he repeated time and again in his polemic with Luxemburg in 1910-11 but it is important to realise that as early as 1893 his discussion of the mass-strike tactic was hedged with similar qualifications, as in a letter to Viktor Adler in 1893 in which he argued that strikes only had a limited chance of success in specific circumstances and when directed to specific ends. To be successful, mass action required a strong, disciplined, class-conscious proletarian political organisation. (Clearly Kautsky did not share Rosa Luxemburg's faith in the 'spontaneous' energy of the masses, a position in which he was of course joined by Lenin.) As time passed, Kautsky's list of preconditions for the mass strike became even longer. On the one hand such a strike had to be 'spontaneous' and could not be decreed by a political party at will. On the other hand it would only be successful where there was widespread and not merely working-class discontent and where virtually *all* industrial workers participated. For this unity, discipline and organisation were absolutely indispensable. In short, mass action had to wait upon the education and organisation of the proletariat.

The organised strength of the Labour movement, however, was not of itself sufficient guarantee of success. For that, the existing regime already had to be crumbling, as, claimed Kautsky, it was in Russia in 1905. This he had already made clear in 1904: 'A strong, far-sighted government which makes an impression on all classes is scarcely to be removed by a political strike'.[45] In 1905, whilst decrying the attempt of *Vorwärts* and the party leadership to stifle discussion of the new tactic, Kautsky nonetheless made clear his view that *German* circumstances were not suitable for its implementation. There had already to be a revolutionary situation before the party could embark upon such a risky course. Just as Bebel had done at the Mannheim party congress of 1906, so Kautsky stressed that the German situation bore no resemblance to that in Russia. For, as he told Luxemburg in 1910, Germany possessed the strongest military regime in the world. Hence he dismissed the Polish revolutionary's vision as utopian fantasy. (Interestingly, Kautsky was joined in the evaluation of the German situation by several whose leftist credentials were beyond question. Trotsky wrote to him in July 1910 that 'Lenin is of the opinion that you are right in your evaluation of the political situation',[46] whilst Parvus, who by no means always saw eye to eye with the editor of *Die Neue Zeit* and who often sided with Luxemburg, was also forced to admit that 'for Rosa the political situation simply doesn't exist'.)[47]

Rosa Luxemburg, on the other hand, was far more optimistic – from a revolutionary point of view – in her assessment of the situation. She had been greatly impressed by spontaneous strike actions in Germany, especially amongst Ruhr miners, in 1905 and even more by the revolutionary upheavals in Russia, where she spent some time in 1906. According to her, German Social Democracy was now faced with a simple choice: either to place itself at the head of the triumphant and swelling ranks of revolution or to be pushed aside by them. Under such circumstances an avowedly revolutionary party could not sit back and do nothing. Hence she launched a tirade against the timidity of the Free Trade Union leadership at the Jena Congress of 1905. 'Doesn't Robert Schmidt see,' she declared, 'that the time has come which our great masters Marx and Engels foresaw, when a period of evolution gives way to one of revolution'.[48] The moment of decision had arrived.

Luxemburg and her former mentor did not only disagree on the prospects of defeat or victory, however. Perhaps even more importantly they regarded the whole question of 'defeat' from totally different perspectives. Although Kautsky had often claimed that the proletariat learnt from its mistakes, although he once claimed that it would arise from temporary setbacks 'like the giant Antaeus' and despite the martial nature of much of his vocabulary (noted by Robert Michels), in the end Kautsky seemed to have doubts about the advisability of any form of action and counselled the SPD to beware of rash adventures. The mass strike was far too dangerous a weapon to be used in misguided experiments and its failure could set the Labour movement back years: 'A defeat in the political mass strike means, if it is fought to the finish, the defeat of all our economic and political organisations and will render the proletariat incapable of struggle for years to come'.[49] Such defeat would cause the working class to lose heart, to mistrust its organisations and reject its leadership.

This caution was a corollary of Kautsky's belief in the importance of organisation and his extremely schematised view of historical development. He saw strong organisation as an essential precondition of successful proletarian revolution (a position from which the party bureaucrats of the SPD could draw succour) and feared that it might be destroyed by premature action. Even in his controversy with Bernstein, when under attack from the right, Kautsky had insisted that his party had no reason to provoke a struggle with the powerful authorities of the Reich. At the turn of the century the working class had a great deal more to lose than its chains and only a fool would provoke unnecessary conflicts which might lead to defeat. In fact Kautsky went so far as to ascribe to the party the job of actually preventing such an occurrence: 'The task of Social Democracy does not consist in hastening the inevitable catastrophe, but in holding it back for as long as possible; that is to say, to carefully avoid anything that might look like provocation'.[50] It was in this respect that Kautsky's position differed most markedly from that of Rosa Luxemburg, who believed that the essence of revolutionary tactics lay in pushing the objective contradictions of Capitalist society to their limit. She did not conceive of the mass strike as a means of achieving limited and specific concessions from the authorities. For her it was only important as part of a grander and more general revolutionary process, only important in so far as it generated revolutionary consciousness amongst the working class. Obviously generalising from the rich experience of the 1905 revolution in Russia, she saw the mass strike as nothing less than the form that proletarian struggle would take in the revolution. Unlike Kautsky, for whom education and organisation were *pre*conditions of revolutionary action, Luxemburg saw class consciousness as a *consequence* of such action, especially on the part of the previously unorganised. Thus she declared at the Magdeburg Party Congress in 1910: 'As soon as we call mighty masses to action in the struggle for suffrage reform, as soon as we organise powerful demonstrations, then soon the masses themselves begin to ask: what more shall we do?'[51] It was important to give the masses confidence in their own ability to resist oppression and exploitation, rather than hold them back from any kind of action and talk down to them.

It was not simply the 'organisational fetishism' of the party and trade-union bureaucrats that Rosa Luxemburg found so distasteful. She had little time for anyone, including Lenin, for whom strict discipline and central control were the hallmarks of revolutionary practice. It was not by erecting a highly centralised and powerful party apparatus that opportunism was to be fought and destroyed. Such a solution was 'artificial' and treated the worker just as the factory supervisor did; as a cog in a machine. It was essential that workers develop their own abilities in action. Organisation, education, consciousness and action were not separate and sequential moments in the revolutionary process but different aspects of the same process. Luxemburg rejected the 'mechanistic-bureaucratic view' which only allowed action when organisation had reached a particular level and insisted instead that 'the living dialectical development gives rise to organisation as the product of struggle'.[52]

This line of argument was quite unacceptable to Kautsky, who repeated that the working class fought to win and not just for the sake of it. It was *successful* action, not any kind of action, which bred proletarian self-confidence. He had difficulty understanding his younger colleague's critical distinction between the *latent* consciousness of the German worker and the *active* consciousness of the Russian. Although at times aware of the danger of bureaucratic stagnation in the party, Kautsky never advocated any tactic to combat the disease and he explicitly denied that a policy of inactive preparation for the glorious but distant day of revolution would lead to inertia.

This difference between Kautsky and Luxemburg only became fully apparent in the bitter debates of 1910 which caused the former much pain and may have led him to a nervous breakdown. But, as we have seen, Kautsky's position was hedged with qualifications from the very start. It had always seen the mass strike primarily as a *defensive* weapon, one to supplement the SPD's parliamentary strategy but never to replace it. The mass strike was the 'last' weapon of the working class, to be used only in defence of democratic rights and then only in preference to more violent tactics. (This of course was also the position of August Bebel and Rudolf Hilferding in both 1905 and 1910-11.)

At this point it is perhaps worth noting that Rosa Luxemburg's view of the mass strike and its potential was not without certain qualification and ambiguities also. Luxemburg did not argue that the mass strike was to replace the SPD's activities in parliament and, although she did talk of 'parliamentary cretinism' at times, she did not adopt Friedeberg's blanket dismissal of electoral participation as 'bourgeois' and corrupting. For her, the mass strike did not carry connotations of necessary violence (though when faced with the realities of revolution in Germany in late 1918 she became more aware of the significance of armed struggle). Above all she denied that it was possible to manufacture a mass strike: 'Such an historical phenomenon as a mass strike cannot be called forth by decree; though equally it cannot be prevented by decree if the time is ripe for it'.[53] Hence the by-no-means totally unfounded charge that Luxemburg was overly reliant upon and trusting in the 'spontaneity' of the masses. Certainly she never really worked out how party organisation and mass action could interrelate and, unlike Pannekoek and other 'Council Communists', Luxemburg never contemplated alternative forms of party organisation to the bureaucratic structures she so disliked.

We have seen that Kautsky's position on the mass strike was ambiguous. Much as he might discuss the tactic at an abstract level, he invariably produced a host of arguments against its use in any particular situation. A similar contradiction informed virtually all his exhortations to revolutionary action. This was even clear to old August Bebel, who said of one of his comrade's most famous articles in 1903, 'He has put the question 'What Now?' [the title of the article], but not really found an answer'.[54] Similarly, Kautsky's seemingly radical *Road to Power* (1909), which predicted wars and revolution, did not match its critical analysis with any suggestions as to suitable *tactics,* as a lawyer employed by the party executive to scrutinise the 'subversive' nature of the text in fear prosecution from the censor's office was forced to admit. The book prescribed only a passive role for the party. Five years earlier Kautsky had seen the alternative confronting the SPD not as 'to fight or not', but as 'to prepare for the fight or not'.[55] He believed at the time that 'our most important practical issue now is less the conquest of power than the conquest of the popular masses'.[56] Such a view characterised Kautsky's political thinking throughout his career. As early as 1881 he wrote that 'our task is not to organise the revolution, but to organise ourselves for the revolution'.[57] Twenty years later he maintained that too many Socialists overestimated the importance of seizing power at the earliest opportunity and overlooked the need for lengthy preparation. Towards the end of his life and in exile Kautsky still refused to advocate armed action against the Nazis and preferred to rely on intellectual/moral *(geistig)* weapons.

There were times when Kautsky *appeared* to be less cautious. Over and over again he stated that violence might be required to overthrow dictatorial rule or defend democratic rights. Even in his controversy with Luxemburg in 1910-11 he maintained that the policy of attrition he advocated (in explicit imitation of Fabius Cunctator of Roman military history) was impossible for the Socialist movements of non-democratic states. Eight years later, in the aftermath of war and revolution, he still insisted that violent revolution had been unavoidable in the military monarchies of Austria and Germany. Yet, having stated this in abstract, Kautsky then performed something of a conjuring trick to dissolve the need for violent action. 'Force' did not necessarily mean 'violence'; it could also mean 'pressure by the majority', organisational superiority or economic indispensability. Although the forces of reaction might try to prevent or destroy democratic institutions, their actions would not necessarily be violent. Recognising the inevitability of defeat, they might give in without a fight and even if they did not, Kautsky could still come up with a store of arguments to justify inaction. A policy of repression was bound to fail against the united forces of a class with 'economic necessity' on its side.[58] This made the total destruction of the organised Labour movement unlikely, especially as such a policy on the part of the Imperial authorities would lead to state bankruptcy and the dislocation of the German economy. Thus the very inevitability of proletarian victory which Kautsky had preached to counter Bernstein's scepticism now became an argument against action demanded on the left of the SPD. An optimistic fatalism (if such is not a contradiction in terms) intruded to excuse inaction in Wilhelmine Germany. It also served to justify passivity in other states at other times. It is intriguing to see how Kautsky used precisely the same arguments to deny the need for violent action in the face of both Communist autocracy and Fascist dictatorship.

After 1917 Kautsky emerged as the leading Marxist opponent of Bolshevik revolutionary practice, which he believed deviated from the true Socialist gospel. In his eyes the Bolsheviks had erected a dictatorship not of but *over* the proletariat. The overthrow of their regime was essential to the fortunes of Democratic Socialism, not only in Russia but world-wide. Thus in 1925 Kautsky appeared to advocate the overthrow of the Russian government by force. Yet the initially brave-sounding call to action ultimately and predicatably disintegrated in the face of familiar arguments: 'objective' economic developments would act in favour of democracy and the refusal of the Bolsheviks to grant democratic rights to the Russian people would create a catastrophe, from which democracy would result. What democratic Socialists should do, therefore, was *wait* for the inevitable upheaval, which might come as a result of Russian military defeat. Precisely the same line of argument was developed by Kautsky in 1934 when he discouraged Socialists (not without sound reason) from immediate action against Hitler, as the circumstances were not propitious. For the moment, what was required was an intensive propaganda effort. In the end and yet again inexorable economic laws would undermine Fascist rule. Even in 1938, so Kautsky confided to Peter Garwy, he naively placed his faith in 'historical optimism'.[59]

Thus Kautsky produced a coherent theory of class conflict which insisted on an increasing gulf between the forces of reaction and those of revolution. But he never went so far as to commit himself to any revolutionary *tactic* in this situation. (In this respect his thinking was typical of that of the Second International as a whole and most unlike the Leninist preoccupation with specific tactics to destabilise and overthrow governments.) For example, Kautsky expressed the greatest sympathy for colonial revolts, yet refused to advocate armed rebellion. When he spoke of class conflict assuming more intense forms, he was not thinking in terms of bloody struggle. In fact class conflict could become more intense and more domesticated simultaneously. Hence Kautsky failed to combine a genuinely revolutionary prognosis wih the advocacy of any form of concrete action. It was this which led the Dutch socialist and former admirer of Kautsky, Anton Pannekoek, to describe Kautskyite theory as 'the theory of action-less waiting... the theory of passive radicalism'.[60] Trotsky was even more scathing in the wake of the October Revolution and Kautsky's criticism thereof, describing the German Social Democrat as 'a very reverend and very useful father and teacher of the church of quietism'.[61] Elsewhere the Russian revolutionary wrote:

> He... resembles to the life a miserable schoolmaster, who for many years has been repeating a description of spring to his pupils within the four walls of his stuffy schoolroom, and when at last, at the sunset of his days as a teacher, he comes out into the fresh air, does not recognise spring, becomes furious (in so far as it is possible for this schoolmaster to become furious) and tries to prove that spring is not spring after all but only a great disorder in nature, because it is taking place against the laws of natural history.[62]

Troksky pulled none of his punches in criticising the man he had formerly revered:

> Kautsky's ship was built for lakes and quiet harbors, not at all for the open sea, and not for a period of storms. If that ship has sprung a leak, and has begun to fill, and is now comfortably going to the bottom, we must throw all the blame upon the storm, the unneces-sary mass of water, the extraordinary size of the waves, and a series

of other unforeseen circumstances for which Kautsky did not build his marvelous instrument'.[63]

If Kautsky's tactical position was ambiguous, no less so was his concept of social revolution.

6   *The state and revolution*

Despite a reticence on the subject of revolutionary tactics shared by most leading theorists of the Second International, Kautsky never doubted that the only road to socialism had to pass through a revolutionary phase. The unfolding of Capitalism's contradictions made social revolution necessary for the further expansion of human productive resources. As commodity production invariably made exploitation and repression the lot of its proletarian victims and as the ruling capitalist class had a vested interest in the maintenance of the prevailing economic and political order, so revolution, not gradual reform *within* the system, was the indispensable precondition of working-class liberation. At the same time, the concentration of capital, the growth of monopolies and state intervention in economic affairs rendered the individual Capitalist entrepreneur superfluous, whilst a massive increase in the productive forces made equality without a generalisation of poverty possible. In this way, and through its production of an ever larger and more self-conscious industrial proletariat, Capitalist society thus prepared the ground for Socialism and its own destruction. Yet Kautsky explicitly rejected the idea that Capitalism would one day reach a point beyond which it could not develop for purely economic reasons. Nor did he share the comfortable belief of several of his revisionist critics that some kind of gradual economic evolution into Socialism – without the pain of *political* revolution – was possible. For Kautsky, Socialism was the product of conflict and above all the conquest of political power by the working class.

According to Kautsky, reforms with the Capitalist mode of

production might result in a marginal improvement in the lot of the worker but that could not produce *qualitative* social change. Labour legislation, won through trade-union struggle, certainly made some difference to the impoverished proletariat but as long as private ownership of the means of production remained, as long as the worker had to sell his labour power to the Capitalist, so – as defined by the theory of surplus value – exploitation remained the order of the day and the labourer did not receive the full value of his labour. As late as 1925 when castigated by the revolutionary left as a 'renegade', Kautsky still maintained that the constant improvement in the worker's position would not diminish the antagonism between Capital and Labour.[64] Reforms were only a palliative, not a cure for the evils of Capitalism. They were important to the Labour movement but only in so far as they strengthened the ability of the working classes to resist oppression by allowing greater time for reflection and organisation.

To Kautsky the existence of democratic rights and institutions was important, for a variety of reasons that will be discussed below. But in a class society the realisation of truly democratic values was illusory. Real democracy could only come *after* proletarian revolution and the abolition of classes. The mere existence of democratic institutions would not prevent the development of increasingly bitter class conflict, though it might make a difference to the particular forms that conflict assumed. According to Kautsky: 'We Marxists are certainly not democrats in the sense that we see in democracy a universal panacea for all the depradations and crimes of society'.[65] In fact the existence of democratic institutions served to heighten class conflict; as in the course of electoral struggles, conflicts of interest became even clearer and class consciousness was helped to crystallise. (This position, incidentally, was not peculiar to Kautsky. On at least one occasion Rosa Luxemburg argued that class conflict reached its most acute form in parliamentary democracy, whilst, perhaps surprisingly, Lenin wrote: 'Economic distinctions are not mitigated but aggravated and intensified under the freedom of "democratic" Capitalism. Parliamentarism does not remove, but lays bare the innate character of the most democratic bourgeois republics as organs of class repression'.)[66]

For Kautsky the state, even in bourgeois democracies, was not the impartial arbiter of Hegelian imagination but an instrument of class rule, hence his hostility to the State-socialist doctrines of Rodbertus and Lassalle and his suspicions concerning Bismarck's social welfare legislation of the 1880s which, he maintained, could never bring about real emancipation. In an age of Imperialism around the turn of the century, Kautsky's view of the state became even more hostile as it devoted ever more resources to Militarism and the building of a battle fleet.

A consequence of this analysis was that social revolution entailed far more than a change in economic relations in the workplace. Nothing less than the seizure of political power could bring about proletarian emancipation. Until that date the SPD had to pursue a course of implacable hostility to the existing authorities. After that date, argued Kautsky, the state apparatus would have to be totally transformed. Above all the proletariat could not co-operate with the old bureaucracy or elements of the armed forces. These points the theorist made not only academically but also in the very real revolutionary situation which the SPD faced in Germany in the wake of the November Revolution of 1918.

Kautsky's prognosis, therefore, was increasingly bitter class conflict, leading to ineluctable proletatian revolution. The mere existence of democratic rights and state intervention in the economy could never heal the contradictions of Capitalism and the realities of exploitation. Yet, just as we have seen that Kautsky's interprepation of the dictatorship of the proletariat was far removed from that of Lenin, so we will find that his critique of the state in Capitalist society was not without its ambiguities, as was his concept of revolution. Kautsky never thought that 'revolution' necessarily entailed violence. 'There are other revolutions than those made with powder and dynamite,' he wrote. In fact it was difficult to predict the precise form that the coming revolution would take and, to a large extent, whether the proletariat would resort to force depended upon the behaviour of its political enemies, a position repeated at times by Rosa Luxemburg, Bebel and other Social Democrats between 1890 and 1914. To the best of my knowledge there was only one occasion when Kautsky spoke of a 'violent political upheaval' and that, significantly, was with reference to the semi-autocratic nature of the German Reich.[67] The essence of revolution for Kautsky was not the particular weapon adopted by the revolutionaries but the conquest of political power by a hitherto oppressed class, which then utilised that power to transform economic relations in its interests. The issue on which Kautsky differed from Bernstein was not that of violence, but rather the *class* nature of qualitative social change.

Furthermore, Kautsky's view of the coming revolution was highly coloured by the prevailing political structures of Germany's Second Reich. If we examine closely his critique of the state and bourgeois democracy, we find that his central preoccupation was the destruction of the German military monarchy, for the Reichstag was not sovereign and hence a parliamentary majority no guarantee of political power or influence. Thus the immediate aim of completing Germany's 'bourgeois' revolution confronted Kautsky and his Social-Democratic colleagues, as well as the ultimate aim of Socialism. This task weighed so heavily on his mind that the more general objections of Marxist theory to the façade of 'bourgeois democracy', objections occasionally repeated by Kautsky, tended to melt away. Thus when he spoke of smashing the machinery of state in 1918 he was not referring to the annihilation of democratic institutions but simply to the end of military-bureaucratic rule. What is more, this could be achieved simply by placing the old civil servants under the control of the democratically elected representatives of the people. In this respect Salvadori is surely right in seeing that the real question of state power was effectively ignored by Kautsky. The same perception was vouchsafed to Anton Pannekoek even before 1914, when in opposition to Kautskyite orthodoxy he stressed that 'the struggle of the proletariat is not simply a struggle against the bourgeoisie *for* state power, but a struggle *against* the power of the state'.[68]

This position was certainly not that of Kautsky, who envisaged the possibility of a state independent of the propertied classes in 1899. As we have already seen he also believed that democratic institutions would as easily be the tool of proletarian dictatorship as of bourgeois rule. What he was saying against Bernstein was sinply that democracy *alone* was not sufficient to end exploitation and class conflict. However, he also criticised Bernstein's blindness to the reality of the Imperial German state. There, what democratic institutions existed were merely the façade for military-bureaucratic rule and this was why a revolution was unavoidable in Germany if Social Democracy were to come to power, not so much to bring about the Socialist millemium as to create a genuinely parliamentary state. There, proletarian revolution was the precursor of democracy and not vice versa. This point he repeated in a letter to Bernstein in 1898 in which he conceded the possibility of a peaceful development to socialism in democratic Britain, yet insisted that a revolution was necessary in Germany to achieve what already existed on the other side of the North Sea. The historically specific nature of Kautsky's objections to supposedly democratic forms of government further explains why his position seemed to change drastically after the Revolution of 1918 which finally brought parliamentary democracy to that part of central Europe. He conceded that the revolution had not fulfilled all his hopes but it had overcome the military monarchy *'whose removal was always the most difficult and most import-ant task for our party'*.[69] Henceforth the problem facing the proletariat was not the conquest but the maintenance of power, and the revolution could be consummated peacefully. (Again it seems to me that Salvadori is right to see Kautsky as a precursor of 'Euro-Communism' in this regard.)

We have seen that Kautsky's conception of revolution was scarcely related to the realism of Lenin and Trotsky, even if it appears more humane in retrospect. Kautsky's revolution would only be violent if the enemy opened fire first. Moreover, that revolution was located at one particular point in time: the overthrow of the German military monarchy. The gap between Kautsky's prognosis and the younger generation of Russian revolutionaries became clear after the events of 1917 (of course). Then the rigid determinism of Kautsky's social analysis widened the gulf between him and the Bolsheviks.

In 1918 Kautsky wrote *The Dictatorship of the Proletariat,* a work which became the gospel of those Marxists who rejected Bolshevik revolutionary practice and which contained possibly the most comprehensive, if also the most tedious, defence of what might be described as the democratic Marxist position. In the years between its publication and Kautsky's lonely death in Holland twenty years later the former editor of *Die Neue Zeit* became obsessed with Lenin and his successors' 'betrayal' of Socialism, a theme developed in countless books and repetitious articles. That critique provoked a distinguished yet bitter response in Lenin's *The Proletarian Revolution and the Renegade Kautsky,* a classic attack on the premises of faint-hearted Social Democracy, and in Leon Trotsky's *Terrorism and Communism.* For an increasing number of Marxist intellectuals and revolutionaries it was the German Social Democrat who had betrayed the heritage of Marx.

The vehemence and hostility with which the leaders of the Russian Revolution castigated Kautsky was not simply the consequence of differing opinions or self-righteous justification. What made the debate so acrimonious was that Kautsky had once appeared as the great friend and mentor of those seeking to overthrow the Tsarist autocracy and adapt Marxism to Russian circumstances. As we have seen, Lenin quoted Kautsky's authority in *What is to be done?* Trotsky did likewise in his earlier writings on the theory of permanent revolution and had an enormous respect for the editor of *Die Neue Zeit,* whose works were widely read in Russian revolutionary circles. Consequently Kautsky's 'treachery' in 1918 was all the more inexcusable in the eyes of his former admirers. It smacked of infanticide.

Prior to the October Revolution Kautsky had shown a much greater and more informed interest in Russian affairs than most of his colleagues. He had developed a number of highly influential ideas. In correspondence with Vikto Adler in 1892 he was already proclaiming the necessity of *proletarian* revolution in Russia on account of the impotence of the native bourgeoisie. But, as the industrial working class there was as yet small, Kautsky saw that the revolutionary intelligentsia, petty bourgeoisie and peasantry would also have an important role to play in the destruction of Tsarism. This idea of a revolutionary alliance of peasantry and proletariat in Russia he continued to develop after the turn of the century, thus preparing the ground for Lenin's polemic against the more conventional ideas of Plekhanov in *Two Tactics of Social Democracy.* In 1905 Kautsky, uncharacteristically, even went so far as to recognise the need for a period of chaos and conflict in which the Russian working class would rise to revolutionary maturity. What was needed was the 'revolution in permanence'.[70] Three years earlier than this, Kautsky had already guaranteed his place in the affections of the left of Russian Social Democracy in a seminal article in *Iskra* entitled 'The Prospects of the Revolu-

Karl Kautsky

tion in Russia', in which he made the following prediction:

> The epicentre of revolution has been moving from the West to the East. In the first half of the nineteenth century it was situated in France, at times in England. In 1848 Germany entered the ranks of the revolutionary nations... Now the Slav... join their ranks and the centre of gravity of revolutionary thought and action is more and more shifting... to Russia. Russia having taken over so much revolutionary initiative from the West may now in her turn become a source of revolutionary energy for the West.[71]

Two years later, in 1904, the German Social Democrat further predicted revolution in Russia as a result of the disastrous war with Japan.

In February 1917 Kautsky's hopes for the overthrow of the *ancien régime* in Russia were of course fulfilled and his reaction was enthusiastic in the extreme. He wrote: 'The Russian revolution is the first ray of hope that has fallen on this poor bloodstained earth since the beginning of the war'.[72] Kautsky even noted that it was the elemental upsurge of the Russian masses, not the disciplined ranks of German Social Democracy, who had realised Engels' dream of revolution. Such praise for revolutionary initiative he did not bestow on the Bolshevik seizure of power in October 1917 when, for the first time, an avowedly Marxist political party came to power.

Kautsky's vigorous hostility to what he considered the opportunistic adventures of the Bolsheviks may have been in part the consequence of a humanitarian dislike of violence. Its heat may have been generated by Lenin's vicious attacks on Kautsky's stance on the issues of war and imperialism, but essentially it was the consequence of the German Social Democrat's mechanistic conception of social change, in which stages of development could not be skipped. The determinism which had constituted a major argument against Bernstein and the Right now enslaved its opponent. The insistence on the inevitability of social revolution and the assurance that Capitalism was creating the preconditions for that revolution now became a two-edged sword, providing a weapon against the radical advocates of direct action. Capitalism created the preconditions of Socialism. Without it and those preconditions, all attempts at socialist construction were doomed to failure.

In fighting against Lenin, Kautsky was reliving some of the struggles of his youth, in particular that waged against the anarchist followers of Johann Most in the 1880s. Any attempt at revolution in an economically backward country he saw as anarchist Utopianism. To Kautsky, Lenin shared precisely such anarchist Utopianism and was a reincarnation of Blanqui and Bakunin. His central objection to Bolshevik practice was summarised in the crass belief that 'revolutions cannot be made but arise out of conditions'.[73] Revolutionary will alone could not surmount the hurdles of economic reality. The realities of production were mightier than the bloodiest terrorism. As a result, Socialism could only be built on the achievements of advanced Capitalism: giant productive forces, an advanced concentration of capital and a large industrial proletariat. (Only where the working class was intellectually and morally superior to the rest of the population and where democratic institutions existed could a minority succeed in establishing a Socialist order.) The absence of these conditions in Russia in 1917 simply meant that the country was 'unripe' for socialisation of the means of production, which was not possible everywhere and under all circumstances.

Again this position was not new to Kautsky's anti-Bolshevik polemic of 1918. In 1895 he stressed that a Socialist economic order depended on an advanced economic structure, as he did again in 1899. Although, as we have seen, he contemplated the possibility of proletarian revolution in Russia after the turn of the century, he at the same time (1904) made it clear that a revolutionary regime there would not be able to introduce Socialism because conditions were not yet 'ripe'.[74] (Significantly, this point of view was shared at the time by Lenin, who wrote: 'The degree of economic development of Russia. . . and the degree of class consciousness, of organization of the broad masses of the proletariat. . . makes the immediate emancipation of the working class impossible'.[75]) Kautsky repeated the point in April 1917: 'There can be no doubt that Russian Capitalism offers few starting points for the development of Socialism'.[76]

Thus the chances of successful Socialist revolution (as distinct from the simple – or not so simple – seizure of power) required giant productive forces and mass support. The use of revolutionary violence to force the pace of historical development was doomed to failure. In fact it indicated weakness and was actually counter-productive, for it caused economic dislocation and constituted a barrier to the self-determination of the proletariat. The destruction of Capitalist property was *not* tantamount to the creation of a Socialist economic order which 'cannot arise from a crippled and stagnant Capitalism, but only from a Capitalism carried to its highest point of productivity'.[77] Revolutionary violence not only bred economic chaos but also civil war. Hence Kautsky offered the following advice: 'Whenever and wherever the working class conquers political power, it behoves us Marxists to ascertain in which normal phase of development this conquest of power has taken place, to make whatever use of this victory is practicable in the given stage of development'.[78] Production had to go on. It was essential that it should not be disrupted. Thus the transition to Socialism required peace and security; it could not be forced by the 'hunger-whip'.

The practices of revolutionary dictatorship and terrorism, however, did more than simply threaten the prospects of a viable economic order. They had dire consequences for the Labour movement itself. Kautsky was convinced that the Bolshevik dictatorship was not a class dictorship but a dictatorship of the Communist Party *over* not just the population at large but also the Russian proletariat. Prefiguring arguments that have since gained wide currency, he argued that a new class structure was emerging in the Soviet Union, in which the bureaucracy formed a new ruling class. The absence of democratic controls would entail the corruption of that stratum and its attempt to remain in power against the wishes of the majority of the populatuon and in an economically backward country would force it to abandon Socialist principles. Furthermore, the absence of democratic structures would prevent the worker from achieving his self-liberation. Only where the worker was the agent of his own emancipation, only where he could act for himself (i.e. in a democratic state), would he finally escape from bondage.

This last and perhaps most interesting objection to Communist autocracy, which bears some resemblance to Luxemburg's famous critique of Lenin's dissolution of the Constituent Assembly, played only a small role in Kautsky's argument however. More usually he was concerned to demonstrate the disruptive effects of violent revolution on economic growth and justify democracy on the grounds of expedience. In fact he insisted that the existence of democratic rights and institutions was essential both before and after the seizure of power for the attainment of Socialism. Democracy and a free press offered the worker the best educational opportunities in Capitalist society and the chance of survival to embryonic Labour movements. They enabled the proletariat to measure its strength and influence – presumably in terms of electoral support – and hence to avoid premature attempts to seize power. The overt existence of political parties with different programmes reflecting their different class interersts served to magnify and make obvious to the man in the street the antagonism of interests between Capital and Labour. At the same time, democratic institutions served to civilise class conflict and increase the prospect of bloodless revolution.

Such institutions were equally necessary after the proletarian seizure of power, both to check the power of bureaucracy and to prevent corruption. Democratic rights and the consequent ability of all sections of the community to participate in the governmental process might win the allegiance of non-proletarian elements, whilst a free press was essential to retain the loyalty of the intelligentsia, whose support was necessary for the successful attainment of Socialism. For Kautsky, therefore, 'democracy constitutes the essential basis for the creation of a Socialist mode of production'.[79]

Such were the arguments brought to bear against the rash and dictatorial exploits of the Russian Bolsheviks. Long before 1918 Kautsky had identified freedom of speech, press and association as far more than a 'bourgeois' platform and had claimed that without them social revolution would be endangered. In 1893 he already saw parliament as the field in which the decisive battle between Capital and Labour would be fought, equating the introduction of real parliamentarism in Germany with the 'political victory of the proletariat'.[80] Again in 1899, the editor of *Die Neue Zeit* wrote in that journal that Socialism was only possible where the proletariat had achieved a capacity for self-government, a capacity it could only develop on the favourable grounds of democracy. Even in 1909, at the same time as the appearance of *The Road to Power,* Kautsky saw parliamentary tactics as indispensable for proletarian emancipation.

It is perhaps worth stressing that this position was common to a large section of the Marxist camp before the Russian Revolution. Rosa Luxemburg claimed that 'the democratic forms of political life in each land... actually involve the most valuable and even indispensable foundations of socialist policy'.[81] In opposition to what she saw as an abuse of power on the part of the Bolsheviks she continued: 'It is a well-known and indisputable fact that without a free and untrammelled press, without the unlimited right of association and assemblage, the rule of the broad mass of the people is entirely unthinkable'.[82] The views of the younger Lenin had not been so different: 'He who seeks to advance towards Socialism by any other road, bypassing political democracy, inevitably arrives at conclusions both economically and politically inept and reactionary'.[83] Perhaps even more surprisingly, Joseph Stalin had this to say of the democratic system in 1901: 'Only such a system will open a free road to a better future, to the unhindered struggle for the establishment of the Socialist system'.[84]

Kautsky thus emerges as a Democrat, convinced of the necessity of the ultimate triumph of Socialism but denying any chance of its early realisation. His huge list of essential preconditions for a successful Socialist strategy – peace, prosperity, weak government, strong and organised proletariat – was so exhaustive as to justify inaction even (or perhaps particularly) in revolutionary situations. Kautsky recognised that poverty and deprivation might generate revolutionary sentiment and that conversely prosperity and constitutionalism might distort working-class perceptions of class antagonism. Yet is was prosperity which made Socialism possible and proletarian victory would stem from the strength of the Labour movement, not the temporary (possibly war-induced) weaknesses of its enemies. This tension between Kautsky's concept of a revolutionary situation and his idea of the necessary preconditions of Socialism explains many of the ambiguities of his theories and not least the distinction between a revolutionary analysis and an almost total silence on the issue of tactics.

7   Kautsky and Marxism

Several salient points emerge from this analysis of Kautsky's political thinking. The first is the general continuity of that thinking throughout his long career, with the signal exception of his position on the question of Imperialism and war. The second is the general ambiguity of Kautskyite theory, especially as far as the question of the state and proletarian dictatorship is concerned. Invariably a seemingly radical analysis was matched by an almost total silence on questions of tactics, about what should be done in the here and now. Thirdly, Kautsky's theory appears as a somewhat mechanistic interpretation of the processes of social change. He appeared to believe that he knew the laws of historical development and that human beings could do relatively little to alter them, hence his extremely cautious approach to questions of revolutionary strategy.

It has often been argued, especially by Russian and East German scholars, that Kautsky's thought underwent a radical change between the publication of *The Road to Power* in 1909 and his attack on Rosa Luxemburg's advocacy of the mass strike in the following year. This view, also shared by Lenin (who dated the change somewhat later, however), of a fundamental discontinuity in Kautsky's thinking is scarcely borne out by what we have already seen. Kautsky himself claimed that those who accused him of betraying his former position had either not read or had not understood his earlier work. Admittedly he modified his position on the issue of capital concentration in agriculture, reformulated his theory of Imperialism and changed his mind on the question of coalition government *after* the revolution of 1918 which ushered in quite new circumstances, but the central features of Kautsky's Marxism remained the same. In 1925 he still clung to the belief in the labour theory of value, capital concentration, class polarisation and increasing class antagonism. Long before 1910 he had envisaged the possibility of non-violent revolution and a democratic dictatorship of the proletariat. His attitude towards the mass strike was always ambiguous and his exhortations to revolutionary action, even in the 1880s, rarely meant more than organisation and education. He had always rejected a voluntaristic model of social change and he continually insisted on the objective preconditions of successful revolutionary action.

At times this constancy produced interesting results. The framework of Kautsky's arguments and his general conclusions would remain the same, yet the justification of those conclusions would change, For example, Kautsky was always suspicious of a policy of peasant protection, so when the theory of a concentration of landownership was shown to be deficient in certain respects, his advocacy of proletarian isolation from the peasantry assumed a different form. The same was true of the thesis of class polarisation. Kautsky held to this to the day he died but the way in which the continued existence of the lower middle class or the emergence of the 'new middle class' was integrated into that thesis varied from article to article and book to book. There were clearly certain theories which Kautsky simply could not bring himself to surrender, though, this said, his defence of those theories was often a match for his opponents, especially in the revisionist controversy.

This is not to say that the emphasis in Kautsky's later writings falls in the same place as in his earlier work. The point is that he was responding to attacks from different directions at different points in time. Clearly his opposition to the anarchism of Johann Most in the 1880s could not take the same form or concentrate on the same points as his opposition to Liberalism and State-socialism. This point Kautsky made himself:

> When I have to deal with a Liberal or a revisionist who denies that the Capitalist mode of production of necessity produces poverty and exacerbates class antagonism, then I deal with the necessary tendencies of Capitalism. If, on the other hand, I have to deal with an anarchist, who denies the possibility of fighting against the impoverishing tendencies in the present mode of production, then I will not concern myself with demonstrating these tendencies, on which we are agreed, but will discuss the successes of the proletarian counter-offensive.[85]

This explains the apparent change in Kautsky's position between 1909 and 1910. His ground was chosen by his opponents and hence his polemic against Max Maurenbrecher's optimistic thesis of peaceful development in *The Road to Power* naturally assumed a one-sided radical appearance, just as his opposition to Rosa Luxemburg's advocacy of direct action in the following year appeared somewhat conservative to the left of German Social Democracy.

Kautsky's theory of social revolution remained fairly constant throughout his life, although one may be able to detect a greater degree of flexibility in the mid-1890s and a greater conviction of the imminence of revolution between 1902 and 1909. It was also ambiguous. Within a revolutionary phraseology, which often borrowed military terminology, was embodied a philosophy of caution. The contradiction between the form and the substance of the SPD's revolutionary theory was acknowledged, indeed criticised, by Eduard Bernstein, disgusted Georges Sorel and has been noted by numerous commentators ever since. That ambiguity, however, was not fortuitous, nor was it a simple consequence of confused thinking. It served a positive function within the SPD and certainly reflected that party's ambivalent position in Wilhelmine Germany. Kautsky came to the Labour movement at a time when it faced a dual threat. On the one hand the anarchist followers of Johann Most, who advocated direct action against the repressive policies of the German and Austrian states, threatened to undermine the unity and organisation of the Socialist movement in its time of crisis. (In the Second Reich the SPD was outlawed from 1878 to 1890 under the terms of the notorious 'exceptional law'). On the other hand, the movement was striving to establish its independent identity and existence against both bourgeois Liberalism and those like Dühring and Rodbertus who looked to the state for salvation. Caught between the advocates of State-socialism and direct action Kautsky was already a centrist. Those who found themselves in a similar situation, such as August Bebel in Germany and Georgi Plekhanov in Russia, developed positions which perhaps predictably repeated the ambiguities of Kautskyite thought.

The ambiguity of 'centrism' was thus in part a consequence of the early experiences of the German Labour movement. It was further encouraged by the peculiar political situation of Imperial Germany, where neither British parliamentary democracy nor Tsarist autocracy was the order of the day. Germany was in a sense a half-way house. There was a parliament, the Reichstag, elected by universal male suffrage yet that parliament was not sovereign. Whole areas of decision-making, especially foreign policy, were the prerogative of the Kaiser, to whom the Imperial Chancellor was exclusively responsible. The attainment of a large number of seats in parliament (and by 1912 the SPD was easily the largest single party in the Reichstag, also winnning approximately one third of the popular vote) was thus no guarantee of political power and influence, from which German Social Democracy was effectively excluded until the upheavals of 1918. It was precisely this situation, combined with discriminatory franchises in the *Länder* (the individual States), the periodic repression of Labour organisations and unequal electoral boundaries which penalised the urban supporters of the SPD, which doomed Bernstein's optimism to failure and which militated against the adoption of unashamedly reformist politics. On the other hand, the fact that the SPD had to compete for votes in more or less free elections gave some impetus to those who wished to abandon the party's isolationism and recruit non-proletarian support. The fact that repression was intermittent, and in the southern states of Germany, especially Baden, relatively rare, together with the ability of the SPD and the Free Trade Unions to develop massive organisational empires and thus a stake in the system after 1890, made the adoption of unambiguously revolutionary politics unlikely. Thus the ambiguities of Kautsky's theory of social revolution mirrored those of German politics before the First World War. Furthermore, the stress upon proletarian independence, combined with a reluctance to advocate direct or immediate action, was equally a product of very real circumstances. The SPD *was* isolated as a significant section of the industrial elite, the lower middle class of artisans, shopkeepers and peasants, and the old landed aristocracy united in anti-labour alliances, such as the so-called 'cartel of productive classes'. The isolation of labour, the fact that the Imperial state could rely not only upon a powerful military machine but also large sectors of the populace against the threat of Socialist revolution, also made sense of Kautsky's caution. Thus his theory was far more suited to the non-revolutionary but repressive situation than the very different kinds of optimism of Bernstein and Luxemburg.

The ambiguities of Kautskyite theory may be theoretically inexcusable but they certainly made a certain kind of sense in Germany before 1914. It was when the situation changed at the end of the First World War, when arguably revolutionary opportunities developed, that the advocates of action came into their own and the old Social Democrat was left by the wayside. The ambiguities or silences of 'orthodox' Marxism, as Kautsky's position had come to be known, also served a positive function for internal SPD politics, helping to unite and give identity to that amorphous group who constituted the party membership. If a theory were to unite South German reformists, pragmatic trade-unionists and Prussian radicals, it had to leave certain things unsaid and the less it said about daily tactics the better. Thus the infamous distinction which Kautsky drew between 'questions of principle' and 'questions of tactics' served to hold the differing groupings within pre-war German Social Democracy together. The stress on inevitable revolution and the Marxist critique of the Capitalist mode of production clearly placed party orthodoxy in the service of the radicals. Yet the emphasis on caution and the centrality of organisation was music to the ears of the party bureaucrats, whose own preoccupation was the maintenance of party unity and the avoidance of unnecessary squabbles. At the same time, the almost total silence on questions of tactics meant that Kautskyite theory did not interfere with the routine work of the party reformists. This was precisely why many on the right of the SPD, such as Theodor Bömelburg, were as annoyed with Bernstein as they were with the Marxist intellectuals. In their view he was simply stirring up trouble and bringing their own activities under the scrutiny of the party left. Best to let sleeping dogs. . .

As we have seen, and as Lenin remarked, tactics were not exactly the strong point of Kautsky's political thinking. In fact his constant stress on man's inability to create 'socialism' at will, his mechanistic view of processes of historical change, lay at the centre of his opposition to Luxemburg's advocacy of the mass strike and Bolshevik revolutionary practice, as we have seen. It was precisely the caution, if not the total passivity, of 'centrist' theory which brought it into disrepute with a younger generation of Marxist theorists who had the good fortune to live through an age of revolutionary upheavals. Trotsky accused Kautsky of 'mechanism',[86] whilst Lukacs charged the Social Democrat with overlooking the 'dialectical relationship between theory and practice'.[87] Such charges were also levied by Georges Sorel, Robert Michels, Rosa Luxemburg, Parvus, Anton Pannekoek and others on the left and by Bernstein from the right. Even the bourgeois politicians/theorists Max Weber and Franz Naumann saw passivity as the hallmark of Marxist 'orthodoxy'. The latter wrote in 1900 that, for the Labour movement, Kautsky's theory entailed the 'danger of falling into a political sleep'.[88]

At a purely abstract level, Kautsky's model of social change was not as mechanistic as many of his contemporary critics and later vilifiers imagined. He drew a clear distinction between determinism and fatalism, insisting that Marxism was not a fatalistic doctrine. He did not deny that fortuitous factors sometimes played a role in historical development, nor that a solitary individual could sometimes change its course. It was a grave error to imagine that the laws of social development operated without human intervention; men did make their own history. Kautsky warned: 'When one operates with the concept of economic necessity one must above all beware of seeing the economic process as a rigid mechanism!'[89] His insistence on the need for *political* organisation, theoretical indoctrination ('consciousness from without') and the seizure of political power distinguished his theory from the more mechanical ideas of social change held by some of the revisionists and, for that matter, by August Bebel, as Hans-Josef Steinberg has shown. Time and again Kautsky pointed out that Marx had not anticipated the automatic collapse of Capitalism as a result of purely economic causes (though he did overlook this himself in some of his writings on Imperialism).

All this is very well, but in practice, when confronted by concrete practical questions, Kautsky often seemed to forget the above. He insisted that Socialism could only be created where Capitalism was highly developed and ridiculed Stalin's policy of economic planning. In the case of Imperial Germany, Bolshevik Russia and the Third Reich, as we have seen, Kautsky did not look to proletarian *action* to solve Labour's problems, but placed his faith in the workings of inexorable economic laws. Attempts to swim against the stream of social development were doomed to failure. Economic laws could not be surmounted by human artifice. 'Inevitability', 'necessity' and even more frequently 'natural laws' and 'natural necessity' were the words which littered Kautsky's writings on every subject under the sun. 'Economic necessity', he declared, 'is the decisive factor in history'.[90] Economic development led with 'natural necessity' to the decline of the small concern.[91] The revolution and the triumph of Socialism were both 'unavoidable'.[92]

The conviction that man was more or less powerless in the face of the 'laws' of Capitalist development and that such 'laws' determined the time and possibility of social revolution was the hallmark of Kautsky's thought. In part this caution and apparent abhorrence of 'rash adventure' may have been a function of Kautsky's temperament. He could scarcely be described as a great activist; the sheer volume of his published work, let alone a quite staggering correspondence with Socialists throughout the world, obviously kept him tied to his desk (though they did not interfere with certain amorous adventures that drove Engels to distraction). As Kautsky himself admitted, even public speaking was not his *forte*. The editor of *Die Neue Zeit* devoted his life to a theory of revolution but its practice and brutalities, as in Russian in 1917 and Germany in the following year, horrified him. Bernstein, who had known Kautsky so well and for so long, declared: 'For you academic work is your prime calling... You go from theory ever more deeply into theory'.[93]

The caution of Kautskyite theory was also a response to the

absence of a revolutionary situation in pre-war Germany, as we have seen. Unlike Tsarist Russia, where the power of the ruling autocracy had been shaken by defeat at the hands of Japan and where a radical intelligentsia and landless peasantry could unite with urban revolutionaries in the overthrow of Tsarism, Germany's Second Reich possessed an efficient and powerful military machine, confident of its ability to repress insurrection. Moreover, a revolutionary struggle in Imperial Germany would have met with opposition not only from the military and bureaucratic establishment but from a much broader section of the community which included big business, the peasantry – already landowning – and the petty bourgeoisie in its ranks, as well as Junkerdom. In addition, the SPD was overwhelmingly a party of the skilled working class. Most women, Polish and Catholic workers, as well as workers in the so-called 'yellow' (company) unions stood outside its ranks, as did the unskilled. Some even belonged to rival organisations. Nor was the SPD united internally, mobilising radicals and reformists, Marxists and revisionists. In such circumstances a frontal assault on the Wilhelmine system would have been suicidal. It needed war and defeat, involving the radicalisation of significant sections of the labour force and the demobilisation of some traditional supporters of the regime, to produce the revolutionary upheaval of November 1918.

All this may explain why Kautsky's orthodoxy enjoyed a certain success in Germany before 1914. However it would be dangerous to see his theory as a mere reflex of the Imperial political scene. After all, there were those in German Social Democracy before the outbreak of the First World War who called for a break with 'passive radicalism'. What made it so difficult for Kautsky to follow this call was the fact that his model of social change was borrowed from the natural sciences or, to be more precise, from a contemporary and bowdlerised understanding of the nature of those sciences. It has been argued often and with considerable force, though rarely with any detailed analysis of the man's writings, that because Kautsky's road to Marx led through Darwin, so his Marxism substituted a naturalistic evolutionism for dialectical understanding and emphasised objective laws of development at the expense of human *praxis*. It cannot be doubted that Darwin's works – or rather crass German formulations thereof – exercised a considerable influence on Kautsky's intellectual development. Whereas Marx and, to a lesser extent, Engels started from Hegel, he started from *The Origin of Species*. Darwin's writings came to him as a 'revelation'[94] and he accepted them with great enthusiasm, though a lot of that initial enthusiasm stemmed from the supposedly anti-religious implications of Darwin's message. Even after Marxism had made its impact on the young Socialist he claimed that Marxism had only 'modified' his Darwinism.[95] When he founded *Die Neue Zeit* in 1883 Kautsky intended that the journal should propagate *both* Marxist and Darwinian ideas.

The influence of Darwin and other theorists of a biologial evolutionism (Haeckel's *History of Creation* and Ludwig Büchner's *Force and Matter*) led Kautsky to stress the unity of the social and natural sciences. In the very first issue of *Die Neue Zeit* he wrote:

> Thus we see that the Darwinist theory of evolution has revolutionary implications not only in the field of the natural sciences. Its effects reach the most distant areas of knowledge and help us understand not only the intellectual life of man but throw new light on the doctrines of political economy and even the laws of our modes of behaviour.[96]

For Kautsky, social science was merely a 'particular area of natural science'[97], and Marx's great achievement had been to unite the two. The materialistic conception of history rested on a recognition of the unity of what happened in nature and society.

This explanation of Kautsky's law-governed view of social

change is not without its critics. Hans-Josef Steinberg, relying on a statement of Kautsky's around 1890 to the effect that he had abandoned Darwinism, claims that the Darwinian influence declined after 1885 and that the 'centrist' was far less mechanistic in his thinking than either Bebel or the revisionists, who often used analogies from evolutionary biology to justify their position. Gary Steenson and Reinhold Hünlich have more recently stressed the non-deterministic aspects of Kautsky's thought and we have already seen that there is considerable evidence *at an abstract level* to support such conclusions concerning Kautskyite theory. He rejected fatalism, stressed that Capitalism would not collapse of its own accord, argued the necessity of political organisation etc. Kautsky himself attacked 'Darwinising' sociologists for arguing from analogies with nature[98] and insisted that social development had its own particular laws and that human beings could transform their environment in a way that plants and animals could not. However, we have already seen that in concrete political situations Kautsky did express a faith in the workings of inexorable economic laws, rather than human action, to overcome dictatorial rule. Although the laws of society might differ from those of nature, such 'laws' nonetheless existed and *governed* human destiny. Thus, even in 1910, Kautsky wrote: 'The difference between nature and society does not reside in the fact that man can alter the one and not the other. The one just as the other confronts him as an overmighty power, from whose laws he cannot excuse himself'.[99] At times, indeed not infrequently, Kautsky might claim that Marxism was only a method, not a list of laws governing the universe. He once even came close to describing the laws of social development as mere explanatory hypotheses: 'Each natural-scientific or social law is an attempt to explain developments in nature or society'.[100] But ultimately his response to Luxemburg, Soviet autocracy and the Third Reich did reveal a mechanistic confidence in historical laws, which he repeatedly described as 'natural laws', as operating with 'natural necessity' and, against Bernstein, Kautsky argued that it was possible to know these with sufficient accuracy to make general predictions about the future. He *knew* that Socialism could not be created in Russia, for all countries had got to go through a stage of Capitalist development. Significantly, Kautsky's rejection of what might be described as Darwinian sociology had less to do with a rejection of scientism as such, was not the result of a recognition that social and natural laws were of quite a different order. It was, rather, a consequence of specific interpretations of and conclusions drawn from Darwin's work, as he made clear in 1885. What is more, some of his objections to what might in the most general (and not the usual) sense be described as 'social Darwinism' were generated less by a universal hostility to natural analogy than by discoveries *within* the realm of evolutionary biology itself, in particular the discoveries of Lamarck. At least, this is how Kautsky once described his intellectual development.

This belief in a law-governed society was common to a whole generation of Marxists for whom Kautsky may stand as a prime example. It was also a belief shared by several revisionists on the right of German Social Democracy, such as Südekum and Grillenberger. Such beliefs, especially the more standard form of 'social Darwinism', were of course not uncommon on the political right at this time either. Whether such belief can find succour in the writings of Marx and Engels, however, is quite a different matter and one which we must now examine.

In the 1920s the Bolsheviks, intent on the character assassination of their most vociferous Marxist critic, published the following remarks which Marx addressed to his daughter, at whom, on a visit to England, Kautsky had set his cap: 'He [Kautsky] is a mediocrity with a small-minded outlook, superwise (only 26), very conceited, industrious in a certain sort of way, he busies himself a lot with statistics but does not read anything very clever

97

out of them, belongs by nature to the tribe of Philistines but is otherwise a decent fellow in his own way'.[101] What the letter really tells us about Kautsky's intellectual debt to Marx, however, is quite a different matter and the Bolsheviks, as their Soviet and East German successors, still continue to believe that Kautsky did give genuine service to the theoretical advancement of Marxism in his 'orthodox' phase (i.e. before 1910 and the dispute with Luxemburg). In any case the letter quoted above was written after only one meeting with Kautsky and before Kautsky had published those works which earned him international recognition as the 'pope' of Socialism. Engels' view of Kautsky may be a better guide for it changed over time. In 1875, when Kautsky first became involved in Socialist politics, Marx's collaborator took an unfavourable view of the writings of a certain 'Symmachos' (a pseudonym Kautsky used at this time) and August Bebel was in full agreement. However, Engels subsequently defended the editor of *Die Neue Zeit* against his critics, entrusted him with a wide variety of tasks and spoke highly of both Kautsky and Bernstein, describing them in a letter to Bebel as 'real pearls'.[102] The draft Erfurt Programme, drawn up by Kautsky, won Engels' praise, as did the Social Democrat's *Catechism* of 1893, a work which has been regarded by some as an early expression of its author's non-revolutionary position, making, as it did, a distinction between a 'revolutionary and a 'revolution-making' party. (According to Kautsky, Social Democracy was the first but not the second.) Engels' subsequent decision to entrust Marx's legacy to Bernstein rather than Kautsky – itself hardly the sanest decision, given the subsequent intellectual genesis of revisionism – should not be seen as the result of any profound intellectual disagreement between Engels and his pupil. It was, rather, a consequence of Engels' disgust at Kautsky's treatment of his (Kautsky's) first wife, who subsequently became Engels' housekeeper.

Obviously, any attempt to assess the proximity of Kautsky's theoretical position to that of Marx cannot rest on the isolated remarks of the founding fathers of 'Scientific Socialism', for both were dead and buried before Kautsky published the great bulk of his writings. (In fact Kautsky lived on until 1938, dying in exile in Holland.) We must therefore examine the substance of Kautsky's writings to ascertain how close they came to the core of Marx's own theory. It is obvious that a vast amount, indeed possibly the overwhelming majority of what Kautsky wrote, was lifted straight from the work of the master. The theory of surplus value, capital concentration and immiseration drew directly on *Capital*, with whose later volumes Kautsky was much better acquainted than most. (Witness his defence of the theory of impoverishment against Bernstein and his refutation of simplistic theories of 'collapse'.) The theory of class polarisation could trace its ancestry to the *Communist Manifesto*. At the same time Kautsky stressed, as had Marx, the necessity of *political* revolution, though his views on the inability of the working class to develop an independent revolutionary consciousness is less easily rooted in Marx's own position. Innumerable other borrowings could be mentioned and when it came to throwing quotations from Marx at intellectual opponents, Kautsky was at least as well equipped as Lenin and Trotsky. A quick survey of their debate on the nature of proletarian dictatorship makes this clear.

Lenin could rely on several passages in Marx's writings to justify his belief in the necessity of violent autocratic rule in the wake of revolution. In his *Critique of the Gotha Programme* (and following earlier but similar remarks in *The Class Struggles in France*) Marx had written: 'Between Capitalist and Communist society lies the period of revolutionary transformation of the one into the other. There corresponds to this also a political transition period in which the state can be nothing but *the revolutionary dictatorship of the proletariat*.'[103] This, as we have seen, Lenin took to justify Bolshevik revolutionary practice, pointing out that in his *Address to the Central Committee of the Communist League* Marx had advocated arming the workers and had proclaimed the necessity of permanent revolution. The *Communist Manifesto* envisaged 'despotic inroads into the rights of property'[104] and at the same time (1848) Marx maintained: 'There is only one way to *shorten* the murderous death agonies of the old society, only one way to shorten the bloody birth pangs of the new society, only *one means* – revolutionary terrorism.'[105] However, this was not all that Marx said on the subject of the revolutionary transition from Capitalism to Socialism and, significantly, Lenin's quotations were drawn overwhelmingly from Marx's writings of 1847 to 1850, when Marx had certain contacts with the French Blanquists and was writing in a revolutionary situation, but a revolutionary situation in a society in which industry was only weakly developed, the industrial proletariat was numerically small and in which democratic institutions did not exist to any large degree. (In short, a situation not so different from that of Russia in 1917, at least in these regards.)

Kautsky came to his 'diluted' interpretation of the 'dictatorship of the proletariat' in quite different circumstances, in industrial Germany. Not surprisingly, therefore, Kautsky quoted not only from Engels' famous preface to the *Class Struggles in France*, which saw the days of barricade revolutions as ended, but also from the writings that Marx produced after his move to industrial Britain. Marx, like Kautsky, always continued to insist that violent revolution was unavoidable in dictatorial states and in the military-monarchies of Germany and Austria-Hungary, but he also stated in a famous speech of 1872 in the Netherlands that the possibility of peaceful revolution through democratic channels existed in states with a large and organised proletariat and in which the political structure was truly parliamentary and democratic. (In this context Marx expressly mentioned the possibility of peaceful transition in Britain, the United States and possibly Holland.) Three years earlier Marx had also reached the following conclusion:

> Universal suffrage is the equivalent of political power for the working class of England, where the proletariat forms the large majority of the population, where, in a long though underground civil war, it has gained a clear consciousness of its position as a class and where even the rural districts know no longer any peasants, but only landlords, industrial capitalists (farmers) and hired laborers. The carrying of Universal Suffrage in England would, therefore, be a far more socialist measure than anything which has been honored with that name on the Continent.[106]

Kautsky's insistence on the democratic aspects of Marx's thinking was thus not without foundation and could also draw succour from Marx and Engels' description of the Paris Commune of 1871 as a form of proletarian dictatorship, for the Commune rested on direct elections and the immediate accountability of all officials. In fact, Marx had no single *model* of revolution, showing a marked historical awareness of the different possibilities in different countries, even in Russia and Ireland, at different points in time. He simply refused to 'write recipes for the cookshops of the future'.

Of course the existence of substantial parallels between the writings of Marx and Kautsky is not of itself sufficient to indicate that the latter had fully understood the former. Indeed, most objections to Karl Kautsky's interpretation of the Marxian doctrine rest more on the general nature, the 'spirit', of his theory of social change than on particular points of interpretation. Thus, although Lenin did swop quotation for quotation with his social-democratic assailant, his main complaint was that Kautsky had robbed Marxism of its 'revolutionary living spirit'.[107] It is such criticism which really hits the fundamental point for, as Kautsky himself remarked on numerous occasions, Marxism was not a set of specific beliefs, not a dogma, but a method of understanding the world in order to change. it. He wrote: 'Of course Marx's words are not a gospel that has to be accepted blindly'.[108] The main charge against Kautsky's interpretation of Marx has been that it confused an essentially critical theory with a positivist sociology modelled on the natural sciences. The dialectical unity of theory and practice, of subject and object, in the original theory gave way to a description of evolution 'according to the laws of the natural sciences'. Such criticism raises a host of problems of course. Precisely what Marx meant by 'dialectics' or the 'dialectical method' is far from self-evident. He never got round to writing the intended book on the subject. Engels said far more about 'dialectics', borrowing the term 'dialectical materialism' (which Marx never used) from Joseph Dietzgen. Yet it is precisely in this respect that Engels is held to have misunderstood Marx's own views, as we will see. However, when Kautsky's detractors speak of his failing to recognise the 'dialectical' nature of Marxian theory they essentially mean the following: the dynamic relationship between man and his environment as expressed in *praxis*, conscious activity to change the world, is overlooked. Kautsky substituted a mechanistic model of social change for an emphasis on the active, revolutionary role of man.

It is doubtless true that the original Marxian theory contained not a few ambiguities. Certainly there are 'deterministic' elements to be found therein, especially when Marx was arguing with anarchists and Utopian Socialists. He certainly never believed that man was free to do all he wanted. Thus, despite the occasional vacillation determined primarily by political considerations, Marx never reconciled himself to the idea that Socialism might come to Russia without an intermediate industrial and bourgeois revolution, though he was admittedly more open-minded than Engels and several later Russian Marxists (Plekhanov and the early Lenin) on the subject. On occasion Marx wrote that no social order perished before it had developed the productive forces of society as far as it could. Men did make their history, but: 'They do not make it under circumstances chosen by themselves, but under circumstances directly encountered, given and transmitted from the past. That tradition of all dead generations weighs like a nightmare on the brain of the living.'[109] Whether such quotations, and the oft-cited comment from the *Preface to the Critique of Political Economy* to the effect that 'Social being determines social consciousness', can be mobilised to support a deterministic interpretation of social change is quite a different matter, however. A fatalistic view of the 'laws' of Capitalist development overlooks the essentially *critical* nature of Marx's stress on the primacy of economic laws in Capitalist society. It was not for nothing that *Capital* carried the subtitle 'Critique of Political Economy'. It was precisely the primacy of economics, the fact that man did not control his own destiny but had become little more than a cog in an economic machine, which Marx was attacking so vehemently. The fact that the worker had become dependent upon and subject to his own creation was the very essence of 'alienation', a concept which Marx developed above all in *The Economic and Philosophical Manuscripts* of 1844 but which, *pace* Louis Althusser, he most certainly did not abandon thereafter. The famous chapter on 'Commodity Fetishism' in the first volume of *Capital* underlines precisely what is wrong both with the reality of Capitalist society and its reflex in bourgeois political economy, namely the fact that human beings are treated and seen as commodities. If the primacy of economics was what Marx saw as the evil of Capitalism, then this had important consequences for his view of revolutionary change. In Capitalist society man was the object of economic laws, not the subject of history, but this did not mean he could do nothing about those laws, otherwise the whole concept of revolution would have had no place in Marxian theory. What it did mean was that man could only escape from those laws by overthrowing the whole structure of Capitalist society and the laws which governed it. Thus, for Marx, social revolution was not simply about the transition from one economic order to another, although it was most certainly about that as well. In the revolution the proletariat would not only be destroying Capitalism but also reasserting control over its own destiny. Only then would 'pre-history' cease and real 'history', with man as its subject not object, become possible. For Marx, the revolution was not simply a determinate act but a process in which man emancipated himself through his own conscious activity. As the *German Ideology* states: 'This revolution is necessary, therefore, not only because the *ruling* class cannot be overthrown in any other way, but also because the class *overturning* it can only in a revolution succeed in ridding itself of all the muck of ages and become fitted to found society anew.'[110] This Promethean concept of revolution was the very antithesis of fatalism. It was *in* action that the proletariat liberated itself, in revolutionary praxis; it was not liberated *by* a determinate act on the part of others, nor only *after* such an act. This was why Marx stated over and over again, 'the proletariat must liberate itself'. It was not simply that no-one else would or could do it, though Marx certainly believed that too. Rather freedom and emancipation could only result from and through voluntary, self-directed action. Such a view is clearly irreconcilable with any mechanistic interpretation of Marxism. Other writings can be mobilised against those who equate Marxism with a theory of economic determinism. When Marx condemned Hegel, he was not only critical of the concept that ideas make history but also of all theories which saw historical processes operating independently of human action. (Whether Marx got Hegel right on this is a different matter that need not detain us here.) In *The German Family* we read:

History does *nothing*; it 'does *not* possess immense riches', it 'does *not* fight battles'. It is *men*, real living men, who do all this, who possess things and fight battles. It is not 'history' which uses men as a means of achieving – as if it were an individual person – *its* own ends. History is *nothing* but the activity of men in pursuit of their ends.[111]

Marx went on to attack 'abstract materialism',[112] whilst his *Theses on Feuerbach* (1845), whatever else they may be, constitute a fierce attack on the strongly deterministic position of the eighteenth-century French materialists. This is especially true of the Third Thesis, which declares: 'The materialist doctrine that men are products of circumstance and upbringing, and that, therefore, changed men are the products of other circumstances and changed upbringing, forgets that it is men that change circumstances and that the educator himself needs educating.'[113]

At a purely theoretical level, as we have already seen, Kautsky conceded that man could achieve certain things through revolutionary action and he rejected ideas that economic developments alone would produce the Socialist society. He was also aware that the transition from Capitalism to Socialism was not simply a transition from one economic order to another but entailed a liberation of man's humanity. Socialism did not simply signify the end of economic exploitation, but the ending of a situation in which human beings had become the 'slaves' of impersonal economic relations.[114] Under Capitalism human relations 'developed independently of the wills of men'[115] and the worker was 'subjugated by his own product'.[116] Under Socialism, on the other hand, men would no longer be at the mercy of impersonal forces but would become ends in themselves. Commodity fetishism would end. Even Kautsky's critique of Lenin rested partly on the belief that dictatorship prevented the worker's self-realisation by depriving him of meaningful activity. And yet, as we have seen repeatedly, when confronted by any specific tactical

105

question the SPD's leading theorist produced innumerable arguments to justify inaction. The proletariat invariably had to *wait* upon the laws of Capitalist develoment. In Kautsky's hands, therefore, Marxism was not, as it was for Lenin, 'a guide to action' but rather a recipe for 'inaction'. Marxism ceased to be a 'philosophy of action' (Antonio Gramsci's euphemism).

Not the least explanation for this state of affairs was Kautsky's equation of Marxism with positivistic science, his belief that social laws were in certain respects akin to those of nature. In this way Kautsky made Marxism approximate more closely to the general run of ideas that were prevalent in the last quarter of the nineteenth century. In that epoch various kinds of 'social Darwinism' held sway, as in Herbert Spencer's *Evolution of Society*. Many looked to the triumphant natural sciences, the bearers of 'progress', to find their model of social change. Some, such as Henri de Saint-Simon, had been doing so since the beginning of the century. (He looked to the Newtonian law of gravitation for inspiration.) August Comte, founder of Positivism, believed that the study of society would soon achieve the same mathematical degree of certainty as astronomy and claimed to have discovered the 'fundamental law which governs the natural progress of civilisation'. This manner of approach to the social sciences persisted at least until the 1890s and became particularly widespread under the abused influence of Darwin's work. Ferdinand Lassalle, founder of an independent Labour movement in Germany in the 1860s, operated with a concept of historical laws. He wrote: 'To want to make a revolution is the foolish idea of immature people who have no conception of the laws of history.'[117] Such fatalistic ideas were not peculiar to the Lassallean elements in German Social Democracy, in which the most prominent ideological stream before 1914 was a form of social evolutionism. Eduard David, Kautsky's antagonist on the agrarian question, saw biological laws at work in society, as did Albert Südekum and Richard

Fischer. In fact, they used arguments from evolutionary biology to counter those who, like Kautsky, believed in the necessity of *political* revolution. But a fatalistic, evolutionary determinism was not restricted to the right wing of the party. August Bebel made frequent reference to Darwin in support of his arguements, believed that 'the stream of development is so strong that it overruns all obstacles'[118] and wrote: 'Society never was something that could be led and directed by single individuals, even if it sometimes looks like that... Rather it is an organism which develops according to its own immanent laws.'[119]

In Kautsky, the inability to appreciate the central significance of praxis in Marxian thought certainly relates to a not dissimilar approach to historical change, although his view was always at the abstract level surrounded with qualifications about fatalism. That inability, however, or at least its roots in a positivistic interpretation of Marx, Kautsky shared with no less a person than Friedrich Engels. Kautsky claimed to have been more influenced by *Anti-Dühring* than any other Socialist work and this is a fact of some significance. For, in *Anti-Dühring*, Engels attempted to apply 'dialectics' to the study of mathematics, physics and all other branches of the natural sciences, as he did even more notoriously (and risibly) in the *Dialectics of Nature*. In his interpretation of Marx, Engels constantly referred to the 'laws' of Capitalist society and likened Marx to Darwin (though it is perhaps only fair to point out that Marx himself was impressed by the work of the natural scientist, to whom he dedicated his major work). According to Engels: 'Marx treats the social movement as a process of social history, governed by laws not only independent of human will, consciousness and intelligence, but rather, on the contrary, determining that will, consciousness and intelligence.'[120]

For Engels, the dialectic was not a question of subject-object identity in revolutionary praxis, nothing to do with the dynamic relationship between man and nature, but was rather a statement of the general laws 'possessing legislative powers with respect to the realms of facts'.[121] For Engels, dialectics reduced itself to 'the science of the general laws of motion, both of the external world and of human thought'.[122] For Engels, 'dialectics' simply meant that 'everything moves, changes, comes into being and passes away'.[123]

Now it is true that Marx himself likened the laws of motion of Capitalist society to natural laws on more than one occasion, although the second and third volumes of *Capital* are full of 'counter-vailing tendencies' and the 'laws' of the first volume are arguably those of an ideal-type model of Capitalism, which Marx certainly did not believe existed in any particular *historical* formation. It is also true that Engels read some of the manuscript of *Anti-Dühring* to his colleague without any objection on the part of the latter. Yet the essentially critical function of economic laws in the Marxian critique of Capitalism, the concept of subject-object unity only through revolutionary praxis, seems to me to be miles apart from Engels's view that certain 'laws' actually 'dispose' of man's affairs as 'God'.[124] For Marx the whole point of revolution was man's reassertion of control over such impersonal forces.

(This interpretation is of course hotly disputed by all Marxist-Leninist commentators, who stress the identity of views held by Marx and Engels. That identity is also emphasised in the later writings of the great Hungarian Communist Georg Lukács, whose own early essays in *History and Class Consciousness* were amongst the first to draw a distinction between the positivistic Engels and the critical Marx. In those days (1923) Lukács denounced any attempt to produce a unitary science of the natural world and human history as un-Marxist and as essentially 'bourgeois' in its consequences, as it overlooked the transformative role of human praxis. More recently a German study of Kautsky, which in

general is most stimulating, has claimed that Kautsky's mis-
understanding of the dialectic cannot be laid at Engel's door.
For, although Reinhold Hünlich recognises the failings of
Kautsky's amalgamation of the natural and the social sciences,
he claims – far too cursorily in this reader's opinion – that Engels'
understanding of dialectics was quite different. In this short space
all I can say is that the case for a distinction between the methodology of Marx and the scientism of Engels is made at some length
and with a good deal of conviction by George Lichtheim, Alfred
Schmidt, Z. A. Jordan and the early Lukács.)

The scientism and positivism which characterised Kautsky's
interpretation of Marx's writings was, as we have seen, part and
parcel of a widespread *Weltanschauung* in nineteenth-century
Europe, which looked to the natural sciences for a model – or
rather many different models – of human history. The 1890s
witnessed a general revolt against this intellectual tradition, a
revolt which came to dispute the ability of man to 'know' or
'identify' *laws* of social development. A school of sociology, often
explicitly anti-Marxist in intent and most famously associated
with the name of Max Weber, emerged which developed a com-
parative methodology, as distinct from a theory of unilinear
development. It was now argued that reality was too complex
and the deficiencies of the human imagination too great to allow
phenomena to be subsumed under general laws. The formulations
of the observer were no more than explanatory hypotheses which
would always be partial and could never be regarded as 'objective'
or 'final' truth. Pareto's 'logico-experimental' method made a
not dissimilar point: 'laws' were not the objective determinants
of social behaviour but simply the hypothetical constructs of
sociologists trying to explain that behaviour. At the same time,
both Weber and Pareto transferred attention from the material
'base' of society to the role of ideas on patterns of social development. Whatever else Weber's *Protestant Ethic* was meant to be –

109

and there is no little dispute on this score – it was certainly intended to refute the primacy of economic factors in explaining the developmentof Capitalism. (Kautsky's monumental but tedious two-volume restatement of *The Materialist Conception of History* in 1927 was in part a response to precisely such arguments.) Similarly, Pareto's theory of political behaviour was written in terms of 'ideological residues'. Bergson's philosophy likewise condemned 'objectivism' and subscribed to a voluntarisitic theory of social change, whilst across the Rhine, Dilthey and Simmel reacted against the earlier 'scientism' and drew a sharp distinction between the worlds of 'nature' and 'culture'.

Such was the general intellectual climate at the turn of the century, a climate brilliantly summarised in H. Stuart Hughes' *Consciousness and Society*. Within the Marxist camp this climate also produce an attack not so much on the work of Marx himself – and in any case even Weber's criticism applies far more, although still often without understanding, to the writings of Kautsky – but upon the 'vulgar' Marxism of the epigones. Bernstein came to deny the 'scientific' nature of Marxism, stressing the limitations of human knowlege, as did the neo-Kantian revisionists such as Kurt Eisner. Bernstein claimed that historical development had reached a stage where human intention was at least as important as material forces and joined the neo-Kantians in an essentially ethical formulation of Socialist commitment, thus prefiguring the later critique of the non-Marxists Weber and Pareto. This rejection of Kautskyite Marxism on the part of the revisionists, who ended up advocating reconciliation with the bourgeoisie and gradual reform within the Capitalist order, was scarcely open to those on the revolutionary left of international Socialism. They too rejected the passivity which seemed to result from Kautsky's stress on objective forces, yet they joined him in his general analysis of the direction of Capitalist development and belief in the necessity of social revolution. Lenin and

Rosa Luxemburg were of the same generation as Weber and Pareto and both attacked schematic Marxism, though Luxemburg's advocacy of the mass strike was markedly at odds with Lenin's theory of the proletarian vanguard. However, as we have already seen, Luxemburg could not emancipate herself totally from the tutelage of Kautsky. Her theory of Imperialism and her trust in the 'spontaneity' of the masses have regularly brought charges of 'mechanism' against her, especially from the Marxist-Leninists, though there can be no doubt that Luxemburg did recognise the crucial role of self-directed action in the Marxian revolutionary scheme. Indeed, she criticised both cautious trade-union bureaucrats in Germany and the Bolsheviks in Russia precisely because their very different strategies stifled proletarian initiative. If anything, the contradictions in Bolshevik revolutionary theory were even more glaring. Both Lenin and Stalin, for example, accepted the Kautskyite prognosis of Capitalism as both accurate and *scientific*, as well as good Marxism. Neither had liberated himself from a positivisitic, scientist view of the world. Lenin saw the materialist conception of history as a 'scientifically demonstrated proposition'[125] whilst Stalin followed Engels and Kautsky in believing that 'the spirit of dialectics permeates the whole of present day science'.[126] At an abstract level both held rather mechanical views of historical development, stressing the 'inevitability' of revolution and the 'laws' which governed human behaviour. (Lenin's later reading of and commentary on Hegel's *Logic* does not fit easily into this interpretation; but then Lenin only came to Hegel late in life.) At the same time, however, and particularly when confronted by immediate tactical questions, the response of Lenin and Stalin was the very opposite to that of their one-time ally: they developed arguments which were essentially voluntarist in nature, expressed on the part of Lenin in the theory of the proletarian vanguard and in the *April Theses* of 1917, which declared the possibility of Socialist revolution in economically underdeveloped Russia, and on the part of Stalin, in the doctrine of 'Socialism in one country'. Lenin mocked the passivity of his Menshevik rivals and ridiculed their schematic view of history, which declared that Russia was only ripe for 'bourgeois' revolution; whilst in his economic planning Stalin stressed the independent and forceful role of the political superstructure in the processes of social change.

At first sight, Leon Trotsky's highly personal and not unexciting formulation of Marxism may seem to avoid this contradiction between a generally mechanistic view of the world on the one hand and an emphasis on the possibilities of revolutionary action on the other. Trotsky expressly accused Kautsky of holding too mechanistic a view of the historical process, as we have already seen, and maintained that 'the resources of history in matters of various possibilities, transitional forms, stages, accelerations and delays are inexhaustible'.[127] For him history did not move along 'a rising line of material and cultural progress'[128] and there was a world of difference between a revolutionary theorist and a 'vulgar' evolutionist. Yet even Trotsky could not divest himself completely of the mantle of 'orthodox' Marxism. He believed that 'revolutions take place according to certain laws'[129] and that 'a popular insurrection cannot be staged. It can only be foreseen'.[130] Early in his career he had argued that the 'logic of history' would thwart the plans of the impatient Lenin[131] and in the bitter years which followed his explusion from Russia after the Revolution and Civil War he still believed that Stalin's rule would prove incapable of surviving the 'laws' of history. In short, there were times when Trotsky's position was as ambivalent as that of Lenin. Even today the prevalent theorists of the Soviet Union subscribe to an essentially scientistic interpretation of Marxism, which has – with some justification – been described as 'neo-Kautskyanism'.[132]

For many the ambivalence of Leninist theory was no real

solution to the dilemmas posed by orthodox Marxism *à la* Kautsky. Some had to abandon deterministic Marxism completely and turn to new philosophies of revolutionary action. Mussolini is perhaps the classic example of this development, though Georges Sorel's theory of the general strike and cathartic, revolutionary violence was also developed in conscious opposition to mechanistic models of social change, which optimistically preached inevitable victory. As Sorel realised: 'The optimist passes with remarkable facility from revolutionary anger to the most ridiculous social pacifism'.[133] He specifically attacked Kautsky's attempt to keep Marxism in a 'rigid mould'[134] and thought it impossible to build a social science by 'generalising the principle of causality borrowed from the physical sciences'.[135] For Sorel, violence was the prophylactic for the evils, corruption and unheroic nature of 'bourgeois' society.

All these responses to Kautsky – and in most cases they were conscious responses to the work of the German Social Democrat – involved problems for a revolutionary Marxist who wished to retain some degree of intellectual coherence. Bernstein's critique chose to forget about revolution. Lenin's combination of a positivistic *Weltanschauung* with tactical voluntarism entailed no small contradiction, whilst Mussolini and Sorel preached a brand of activism which both theoretically and in practice seemed to sacrifice the proletariat to their own self-fulfilment. For this reader, only one critique of Kautsky's Marxism preserved the core of Marx's message without theoretical confusion. This was a critique which was less concerned to throw individual quotations at ideological enemies then to unravel the essentially critical spirit of Marx's original work and which identified the concept of *praxis* as its heart. That critique found its most distinguished representatives in the Austrian Karl Korsch, the Hungarian Georg Lukács and, to a lesser extent, the Italian Antonio Gramsci. These, especially Korsch and Lukács, came to Marx through Hegel (of whose work Kautsky was essentially ignorant), not Darwin. Korsch laid great emphasis on the Hegelian origins of Marx's ideas, stressed the difference between those ideas and the 'natural-scientific materialism' of Kautsky [136] and believed Marxism to be a 'critical' rather than a 'positive' science. [137] Regarding the eleventh thesis on Feuerbach ('Philosophers have only interpreted the world. The point however is to change it!') as the key to Marxian theory Korsch saw that Marx viewed social development 'not only as an objective, historical process of becoming, but at the same time as subjective, historical action, "revolutionary, practical-critical activity" or "transforming praxis"'. [138]

For Lukács, influenced significantly by Sorel amongst others and by the Heidelberg school's rejection of Positivism, Marxism was essentially a critical theory which relied on proletarian praxis to make the social revolution. In his eyes natural-scientific ideologies misrepresented Marx and were instruments of bourgeois ideological hegemony (to borrow Gramscian terminology). Hence Lukács could not stomach the 'dialectical materialism' of Kautsky. It was Lukács in particular, partly under the influence of Rosa Luxemburg's work, who argued that for Marx the revolution was not one determinate act but a series of actions, a *process* of struggle, in which the proletariat came to maturity, became conscious of its historical mission and began to reassert control over its own destiny. For Lukács the revolution was nothing but 'the process of educating the proletariat'[139] and this was why at least the earlier essays in *History and Class Consciousness* (1923) saw the workers' council as the organisational form of the revolution.

This interpretation of Marx gave Korsch and Lukács the opportunity to attack Kautsky on the basis of Marx's own work and not tactical expedience. A policy of caution, of *waiting* upon historical developments, was in fact an aspect of *alienation*, of being at the mercy of impersonal economic forces, whereas the whole point of revolution was the liberation of man from those impersonal forces. Yet it seems to me that Lukács and Gramsci, who also saw Marxism as a 'philosophy of action' and advocated workers' councils, both contradicted an initial vision of proletarian self-liberation through workers' councils by their veneration of Lenin and by the adoption of the theory of the vanguard party. Such veneration is certainly not difficult to understand. Lenin had made a revolution, had succeeded where Kautsky and German Social Democracy had failed. The more the threat of Socialist revolution receded in Western Europe, the more the Bolshevik model gained in plausibility. But, unfortunately, that model placed in jeopardy the whole concept of proletarian praxis. If the point of revolution in Marx's scheme was the worker's reappropriation of his own fate, was his self-directed action, then it is difficult to see how subjection to a professional revolutionary elite can be equated with that revolution. In those terms the revolution of the vanguard party entails only the liberation of its own favoured members.

This Korsch, following Luxemburg, realised. Hence he attacked both Social Democracy and Bolshevism with the tools of Marx's own revolutionary concepts. Yet the fate of Luxemburg (murdered by counter-revolutionaries in the Spartacist uprising of January 1919 in Germany) and of Korsch (who was active in left-Communist groupings in Germany in the 1920s but ultimately emigrated to the United States of America) warn against too great an admiration of their Promethean revolutionary vision. Unlike Lenin they were not successful in seizing power. On the other hand, it is more than a little doubtful that the Bolsheviks realised anything resembling Marx's view of Socialism and human freedom in the admittedly unfavourable circumstances of Russia. In a sense Kautsky was right: to seize power is one thing, to build a humanitarian Socialism another.

8   Reflections

Any attempt to assess the validity of Kautsky's view of Capitalism and its future development is rendered difficult, not only by the generality of that theory and its ambiguities but also because its author was not an academic working within what were once the comfortable groves of academe. He was the theorist of a revolutionary party, of a mass movement, and he saw his task as the popularisation of Marxism and the furtherance of social revolution. Kautsky was well aware that in popularising Marx's writings he was also guilty of simplifying and vulgarising the ideas of the master and consequently a sophisticated and painstaking critique of his thought may easily miss the point. His theory aimed at achieving a concrete political goal (the seizure of political power by the industrial working class) and it may be questionable whether 'objectivity' was or was not intended. However, in so far as Kautskyite theory dispensed with the more 'philosophical' aspects of Marxism and concentrated on what might be described as Marxist 'sociology', in so far as Kautsky did believe that he had produced a coherent and *verifiable* model of social development, then a partial critique thereof may not be completely out of order. This is especially so as the failure of Social-Democratic tactics to produce a genuinely Socialist revolution was at least in part related to the deficiencies of vulgar Marxism. What is more, the subsequent development of other revolutionary theories rested precisely on a critique of Kautsky's theoretical failings. It is therefore not improper to ask precisely where Kautsky went wrong.

Any discussion of Kautsky's theory of social revolution has to begin with the painful fact that Social-Democratic tactics (social *revolution* via a parliamentary majority in a genuinely democratic state) have nowhere succeeded. This is not to say that the existence of democratic rights and institutions has brought Labour no benefits, especially where a strong Labour movement has existed. Indeed, it is possible to argue that the combination of these factors, most obviously in Sweden but also in many other European states, has led to a change in the quality of life for the wage-labourer. The welfare state and its benefits to the more disadvantaged sections of society are certainly not to be scoffed at but victories in the realm of distribution, at present under threat by conservative forces in Europe, are not tantamount to the social revolution which Kautsky and his colleagues predicted. In the Western Democracies the means of production have sometimes and partially been nationalised, but *not* socialised. The logic of production remains profit, exchange not use. Nowhere has the proletariat been able – or even in most cases wanted – to use its influence to expropriate the expropriators once and for all.

In part, the failure to implement social revolution in Western Europe has been a result of the integrative tendencies of democratic structures, of which Kautsky appears to have been blissfully unaware. It would seem that the existence of democratic rights, the extension of the rights of 'citizenship' to the working class, does impinge on the conduct and perception of class struggle even where – and that is everywhere – gross inequalities in income and the distribution of real power and influence continue to exist, just as T. H. Marshall claimed in *Class, Citizenship and Social Development*. As I have argued at length elsewhere, the genesis of a *political* class consciousness on the part of the industrial working class has been no simple reflex of economic struggle, nor for that matter, *pace* Kautsky and Lenin, of the existence of a revolutionary intelligentsia. Rather it has been the result of state policies, especially of discrimination and repression. Significantly the revolutions that have taken place in the last two centuries – the Russian Revolution of 1917 and the German Revolutions of 1848 and 1918, as well as innumerable colonial revolts (military coups aside) – have been movements to extend citizenship rights, even if they were *also* Socialist in inspiration. Class antagonisms thus seem to assume more serious contours and culminate in Social revolution more often in non-democratic than democratic societies. The point was noted long ago by Georges Sorel, who wrote: 'Experience teaches us that democracy can work effectively to hinder the progress of Socialism',[140] whilst Hendrik de Man also saw revolutionary Socialism as a product of non-democratic structures. It would seem that participation on the part of the Labour movement in democratic processes of government does not prepare Labour for the social revolution, as Kautsky imagined, but serves to de-fuse revolutionary momentum. That participation can lead to an acceptance of the 'rules of the game', an acceptance of prevailing political norms and a renunciation, or at least forgetting of the revolutionary goal. The day-to-day pressure of attracting votes and parliamentary manoeuvre become ends in themselves and cease to be merely the preconditions of more sweeping social change. Precisely this point was made by a group of young radicals at the SPD party congress of 1891 and repeated by Friedeberg in the mass-strike debate. It also informed Rosa Luxemburg's worries on the score of 'parliamentary cretinism' and led Parvus to write: 'Thus parliamentarism confronts Social Democracy with many small, practical tasks, which easily lead away from the road of principled opposition to the Capitalist state and even more easily mislead the observer.'[141] Thus the existence of democratic forms of government does not necessarily favour the development of revolutionary consciousness on the part of the proletariat and may even be said to hinder it *in certain situations*. This last qualification is crucial, however. Kautsky never claimed that the mere existence of democratic structures led necessarily to the triumph of Socialism. Their efficacy in this regard depended upon other factors, upon the existence of a large, powerful, united and class-conscious Labour movement. The polarisation of the class structure and the resultant class conflict was central to the success of Socialism, as already noted. As a result Kautsky might argue that the failure of Socialist revolution in Germany was a consequence of division within the Socialist ranks, whilst the absence of revolutionary initiatives in industrial Britain could be laid at the door of ideological weaknesses and the absence of revolutionary theory and consciousness. Yet such claims do *not* serve to counter arguments about the integrative consequences of democratic structures, for ideological purity and participation in the democratic process seem to be dependent not independent variables. Nor are ideological purity and proletarian unity the most compatible of things. This was a problem Kautsky had to confront regularly in his own party.

The list of preconditions which Kautsky drew up for successful revolutionary action involved not only the 'maturity' of economic factors, but also a subjective element, namely the 'maturity' of the revolutionary class, the proletariat. The substance of that maturity was organisation, unity, discipline and class consciousness. Yet, as we have seen, revolutionary consciousness was not the automatic reflex of economic struggle or trade-union action. It was precisely the task of the party, of Social Democracy, to awaken revolutionary consciousness, inspire the working class with great aims, and imbue it with Scientific Socialism. To this end the party clearly had to be on its guard against ideological deviance. As a result Kautsky played a prominent part in the removal of the revisionist Kurt Eisner from the editorial board of *Vorwärts*, the party's central organ, in 1906 and in a letter of 14 November 1894 to Bernstein he advocated that Vollmar be expelled from the party on account of his reformist beliefs. His correspondence with Viktor Adler after the Dresden party conference of 1903, at which revisionism was overwhelmingly condemned, also expressed disquiet that the SPD executive had not acted more vigorously against the heretics. It was such views which brought Kautsky into disrepute amongst the ranks of the reformists, who in general prefered to avoid ideological debate. Eduard David once asked, 'why don't you try to understand the views of your opponents for once?'[142] whilst Wolfgang Heine and Vollmar both accused the editor of *Die Neue Zeit* of dogmatism. The latter dismissed Kautsky as a 'theoretical fanatic' and as a 'Professor who would rather let the world and the party go to the dogs than let one brick be removed from the edifice of his doctrine'.[143]

However, Kautsky's insistence on party discipline, which like that of the party leadership at this point in time was almost exclusively directed at the right, especially the reformist SPD *Landtag* delegations in Baden, Bavaria and Hessen, was again not without its ambiguities. In fact, in order to preserve party unity he was prepared to make significant concessions. Thus he normally stopped short of demanding the expulsion of revisionists and reformists from the ranks of Social Democracy. Kautsky left it to the individual conscience of the party member to decide whether his views accorded with those of the party programme. In any case – and here again the old fatalism surfaces – the existence of two ideological streams within German Social Democracy was inevitable and reformism was only an 'episode',[144] one which would soon be rendered obsolete by historical circumstance, as the masses themselves were not revisionist or reformist in orientation. (These deviations Kautsky regularly ascribed to 'petty-bourgeois' elements within the Socialist movement.) Thus Kautsky could not draw the logical conclusion, which Lenin did draw: if ideological purity were crucial for the prospects of revolution, then the impure had to be booted out of the ranks of the party. This is one of the reasons why Kautsky made innumerable attempts to bring the Bolshevik and Menshevik wings of Russian Social Democracy together again after the split of 1903 and why the division of the German Labour movement during the First World War caused him such anguish. In short, ideological purity and proletarian unity are not the most compatible of things and it is more than a little debatable whether a high degree of ideological commitment and a *mass* organisation are compatible. In a sense unity in the SPD was purchased at the expense of theoretical purity; or as Lenin put it: 'The proletariat's right to revolution was sold for a mess of potage in the shape of organisations permitted by present police law.'[145]

(I do not intend by this that Kautsky deliberatly constructed his theory in such a way as to 'integrate' the various and conflicting wings of German Social Democracy, as Erich Matthias once argued. Rather, as Hans-Josef Steinberg and Reinhold Hünlich have pointed out, Kautsky was prepared to criticise the party executive and *Vorwärts* for attempting to stifle controversy. However, as argued earlier, the nature of Kautskyite theory, by its silence on tactics and stress on organisation, did 'objectively' serve an integrative function.)

That very stress on the importance of organisation and discipline whilst *waiting* for the great day to dawn may also have served to diminish revolutionary potential. Occasionally Kautsky recognised that the reformist position of the Free Trade Unions in the mass-strike debate of 1910-11 was a consequence of their financial and organisational assets, which they did not wish to put at risk. Between 1910 and 1914 he also expressed some disquiet at the bureaucratic tendencies of his party, although he never conceived of how they might be countered, except by theoretical commitment. But in the main and as we have seen over and over again Kautsky was a firm believer in the importance of strong organisation. This entailed certain problems. Even before 1914 and in a manner not dissimilar to Rosa Luxemburg's critique of the SPD and trade-union leadership, the sociologist (and one-time friend of Kautsky) Robert Michels claimed that the bureaucratic organisation of mass movements, as advocated by the SPD's leading theorist, led inevitably to oligarchic rule and increasing influence for bourgeois, non-revolutionary, bureaucratically minded leaders. He wrote: 'Organization is in fact the source from which the conservative currents flow over the plain of democracy.'[146] Significantly, the model for this thesis was none other than the German Social Democratic Party, of which Michels was once an uneasy member (being rather more impressed by the aesthetics of active anarchism). When applied to the SPD the thesis is certainly not without a degree of justification. From 1907 a new kind of organisation-man, epitomised by Freidrich Ebert, emerged as a significant force in the party. Although at this stage not unreservedly on the right of the party, Ebert nonetheless symbolised the bureaucrat's desire to avoid 'unnecessary' theoretical squabbles and keep the party united. Subsequently, of course, he was to play, as the leader of the Majority Social Democratic Party, an essentially counter-revolutionary role in the upheavals of November 1918 in Germany, in which he declared that he hated revolution 'like sin'. The creation of bureaucratic structures to organise mass movements may also lead to excessive caution not only because of the kind of leadership it produces (a leadership, which according to Michels became increasingly petty-bourgeois in its objective as well as subjective situation, enjoying relatively high wages and job-security), but also because the maintenance of organisation becomes an end in itself. A process of 'goal displacement' takes place, in which the initial goal (social revolution) is increasingly forgotten and organisational imperatives become uppermost. This would seem to explain, amongst other things, why the Free Trade Unions were so cautious on the question of the mass strike and was certainly one of the reasons why the leadership of the SPD sought to avoid a confrontation with the German government on the outbreak of the First World War. It is also true, as Peter Nettl pointed out, that there was a decline in internal party democracy between 1910 and 1914, with conferences and conference agenda becoming increasingly – though far from completely – stage-managed.

There may thus be *some* truth in Michel's thesis, at least as far as the *national* party leadership is concerned. As I have argued at length elsewhere, however, that thesis is most problematical. The SPD, even in the years of the Anti-Socialist Law, was never uniformly revolutionary, any more than the party, or even the party leadership, was uniformly reformist in 1914. Thus no unilinear process of goal displacement took place. The degree of bureaucratisation of party and unions is easily exaggerated, as Klaus Schönhoven and Gerhard Beier have shown, whilst few party bureaucrats enjoyed living standards *significantly* superior to the party's skilled rank and file. Despite bureaucratisation some party branches remained radical, whilst the strength of reformist elements in the party was less a consequence of organisation as such than the specific form of Social-Democratic organisation before 1914, which grossly underrepresented the radicals from the large cities. In short, organisation does not *necessarily* produce conservatism, though some aspects of the caution of the SPD leadership may legitimately be ascribed to bureaucratic stagnation.

It is not clear, therefore, that the strategy advocated by Kautsky of unity and organisation necessarily had a counter-revolutionary import, though it may have served to compromise the development of a revolutionary consciousness. Where Kautsky's prognosis of Social-Democratic revolution really came unstuck was in its reliance on the polarisation of class antagonism, both objectively and subjectively. Even before 1914 Kautsky believed that the proletariat had become the largest and most significant class in Capitalist society and, whatever he might say in his theory of 'consciousness from without' concerning the acquisition of Scientific Socialist principles, he had no doubt that the class 'instincts' of the proletariat would indicate to it where it stood in the class struggle. This involved two serious flaws. In the first place, class 'instincts' were as often absent as present, if by them one means commitment to class *struggle* as distinct from an awareness of a difference between 'them and us', an awareness which is of course compatible with any number of different political positions. In the second place, Kautsky continually overestimated the numerical strength and internal solidarity of the proletariat. In Germany in 1914 approximately one third of the active population earnt its living from agriculture and, although landless labourers may count as 'proletarians', few were unionised and even fewer gave their support to the SPD. Of those engaged in industry and handicrafts, approximately one third were self-employed or worked in very small firms employing no more than five people in 1907. Whole sectors of German industry were characterised by domestic outwork: textiles in the villages of Saxony, Thuringia and North-East Franconia, shoe-making in Pirmasens and the leather, wood, instrument and toy-making industries in general. In short there was a large group of 'workers' outside the factories. At least a half of them were also outside the large towns, living in towns and villages of under 10,000 inhabitants. Yet the recruits of the Labour movement came overwhelmingly from the large, indeed the largest, cities of Protestant Germany: Berlin, Hamburg, Dresden and Leipzig.

This last point raises another: even the factory proletariat of the large industrial towns was more fragmented in its allegiances than Kautsky cared to imagine. Catholic unions and adherence to the Catholic Centre party characterised the working class of Aachen, Cologne and much of South Germany and Silesia. Poles formed their own unions and political parties. In coal, iron, steel, chemicals, and the electrical industry a significant percentage of the labour force belonged to company unions and seemed to shun the Social-Democratic struggle. Few unskilled workers were organised at all and even fewer women. The significant growth of a white-collar salariat further complicated the situation, constituting by 1925 approximately twenty per cent of the German labour force.

Thus even in Wilhelmine Germany, a society whose contours were arguably more determined by *class* antagonisms than many others, many wage-labourers failed to identify with the Socialist movement. The same has remained true to this day, whilst the numerical size of the industrial labour force in advanced industrial countries has shrunk with the spectacular growth of the service sector and high levels of unemployment in manufacturing. Thus the twin props of Kautsky's prediction of social revolution without revolutionary dictatorship have crumbled.

A further problem concerns the continued power and hegemony – not only physical – of the bourgeoisie. Significantly, successful seizures of power on the part of Marxist revolutionaries have taken place in countries with a weak indigenous bourgeoisie (Russia, China, Cuba and most colonial revolutions). In the industrial societies of the West the situation has been very different. The petty-bourgeoisie and peasantry have often shown themselves to be allies of anti-Socialist forces, especially in the inter-war period, though not always, whilst the industrial bourgeoisie possesses a power and ideological influence which reaches way beyond the factory gate. The conclusion is that revolutions are *less*, not more likely in industrial societies. This is so for another reason, one identified by Engels long ago. The modern state has immense sources of social control at its fingertips, from social-welfare benefits to blind (or increasingly better-informed) repression. The existence of standing armies, the immense cost of the modern technology of warfare and even the physical layout of modern cities weights the scales in favour of the forces of 'order' and against the private citizen.

The problems of Kautsky's theory reach even further, of course. Like most Marxists of his generation he arguably underplayed the hegemony of bourgeois ideology and even more seriously underestimated the role which the political 'super-structure' can play in the determination of social processess. Yet the point is perhaps that Kautsky was precisely typical of that generation, that his faults were not that individual. Certainly his assessment of the German situation before 1914 was more realistic than that of most of his critics, came they from the left or the right. His defence of the Marxian theories of immiseration and Capitalist crisis were in fact less mechanical and truer to Marx than much ill-informed criticism (still to be found today). His predicitions of class conflict, revolution and war were hardly inaccurate in the Europe of 1890-1930. His failure was the failure of democratic Marxism *everywhere*.

Notes

1 *The Labour Revolution* (London, 1925), p. 266.

2 *Die Gesellschaft,* 1 (1927), p. 67; also *Karl Marx' Ökonomische Lehren*, 12 ed (Stuttgart, 1908), p. 88.

3 *Die Neue Zeit* (henceforth *NZ*), 35 (1917), 1, p. 292.

4 Vladimir Akimov, 'The Second Congress of the Russian Social Democratic Party' (1904), in Jonathan Frankel (ed), *Vladimir Akimov on The Dilemas of Russian Marxism, 1895-1903* (Cambridge, 1969), p. 150.

5 *Der Kampf*, 14 (1921), p. 277.

6 Kautsky to Adler 5 May 1894, in Friedrich Adler (ed), *Viktor Adler. Briefwechsel mit Karl Kautsky* (Vienna, 1954), p. 152.

7 *NZ* 19 (1901), 1, p. 37.

8 *NZ* 25 (1907), 1, p. 339.

9 *NZ* 19 (1901), 2, p. 90.

10 *NZ* 20 (1902), 1, p. 80.

11 *NZ* 27 (1909), 1, p. 45.

12 *NZ* 18 (1900), 1, p. 200.

13 Quoted in Peter Gay, *The Dilemma of Democratic Socialism: Eduard Bernstein's Challenge to Marx* (London, 1962), p. 250.

14 J. P. Nettl, *Rosa Luxemburg* (Oxford, 1966), Vol 1, p. 204.

15. Rosa Luxemburg, *Politische Schriften* (Leipsig, 1969), p. 94.

16 Bernstein, *Evolutionary Socialism* (London, 1909), p. x.

17 Bernstein, *Zur Theorie und Geschichte des Sozialismus,* 4 ed (Berlin, 1904), pt 2, p. 9.

18 *NZ* 21 (1903), 2, p. 751.

19 Luxemburg, *Politische Schriften,* p. 13.

20 George Lichtheim, *Marxism. A Historical and Critical Study* (London, 1964), p. 265f.

21 Quoted in Israel Getzler, *Martov. A Political Biography of a Russian Social Democrat* (Melbourne, 1967), p. 53.

22 *Mein Lebenswerk,* reproduced in Benedikt Kautsky (ed), *Ein Leben für den Sozialismus* (Hanover, 1954), p. 23.

23 Kautsky to Bernstein 10 June 1898, in International Institute for Social History (Amsterdam), Kautsky Nachlass (KA) c 193.

24 Kautsky to Bernstein 30 August 1897, in KA. c 175.

25 Quoted in Hélène Carrère d'Encausse and Stuart R. Schram, *Marxism and Asia* (London, 1969), p. 161.

26 Nettl, Vol 2, p. 527.

27 *NZ* 20 (1902), 2, p. 138.

28 See the minutes of *VIIe Congrès Socialiste Internationale* (Stuttgart, 1907), p. 314.

29 *Der Erfurter Programm* 4 ed (Stuttgart, 1902), p. 11f.

30 *NZ* 4 (1886), p. 544.

31 *NZ* 16 (1898), 1, p. 806.

32 *Ibid.* p. 810.

33 Thus Bebel at the Stuttgart Congress of the Second International: *VIIe Congrès,* p. 114.

34 *Handelspolitik und Sozialdemokratie. Populäre Darstellung der handelspolitischen Streitfragen* (Berlin, 1901), p. 91.

35 *NZ* 30 (1912), 2, pp. 845-51.

36 Quoted in Gustav Noske, *Kolonialpolitik und Sozial-demokratie* (Stuttgart, 1914), p. 56.

37 *NZ* 31 (1913), 2, p. 444.

38 *NZ* 32 (1914), 2, p. 921.

39 Quoted in Carl E. Schorske, *German Social Democracy* (Cambridge, Mass., 1955), p. 199.

40 Quoted in Hans-Christoph Schröder, *Sozialismus und Imperialismus. Die Auseinandearsetzung der deutschen Sozialdemokratie mit dem Imperialismusproblem und der 'Weltpolitik' vor 1914* (Hanover, 1968), p. 115.

41 Lenin, *Imperialism. The Highest Stage of Capitalism* (Moscow, n.d.), p. 243.

42 *The Social Revolution* (London, 1909), p. 47.

43 *VIe Congrès Socialiste Internationale* (Amsterdam, 1904), p. 51.

44 *Social Revolution,* p. 44.

45 *Der politische Massenstreik* (Berlin, 1914), p. 95.

46 Trotsky to Kautsky 21 July 1910, in KA DXXII 168.

47 Parvus to Kautsky 14 June 1910, in KA DXVIII 462.

48 *Protokoll über die Verhandlungen des Parteitages der Sozialdemokratischen Partei Deutschlands. Abgehalten zu Jena vom 17. bis 23. September 1905* (Berlin, 1905), p. 320.

49 *Le Marxisme et son critique Bernstein* (Paris, 1900), p. xii.

50 *Protokoll. . . Magdeburg 1910* (Berlin, 1910), p. 427.

51 Rosa Luxemburg, *Massenstreik, Partei, Gewerkschaften* (Leipzig, 1919), p. 46.

52 *Protokoll. . . Magdeburg,* p. 428f.

54 Quoted in Jürgen Kuczynski, *Die Geschichte der Lage der Arbeiter unter dem Kapitalismus* Pt 1 (Berlin, 1962), Vol 4, p. 171.

55 *NZ* 22 (1904), 2, p. 581.

56 *NZ* 22 (1904), 1, p. 1.

57 *Der Sozialdemokrat* no. 8 (1881), p. 1.

58 *NZ* 25 (1907), 1, p. 461.

59 Kautsky to Peter Garwy 27-30 August 1938, in KA c 427. See also Kautsky to A. H. Gerhard 8 April 1938, in KA c 428.

60 *NZ* 30 (1912), 2, p. 694.

61 Leon Trotsky, *Terrorism and Communism* (Ann Arbor, 1963), p. 183.

62 Leon Trotsky, *Permanent Revolution and Results and Prospects* (London, 1962), p. 167.

63 Trotsky, *Terrorism,* p. 88.

64 *Labour Revolution,* p. 147.

65 *Die Wurzeln der Politik Wilsons* (Berlin, 1919), p. 32.

66 Lenin, *Selected Works* Vol 1 (Moscow, 1950), Pt 1, p. 93.

67 See Hans-Josef Steinberg, *Sozialismus und Sozialdemokratie* (Hanover, 1969), p. 80f.

68 Quoted in Iring Fetscher, *Der Marxismus* (Munich, 1965), Vol 3, p. 334.

69 Kautsky's own emphasis. Karl Kautsky, *Texte zu den Programmen der Sozialdemokratie* (Cologne, 1968), p. 278.

70 *NZ* 23 (1905), 2, p. 462.

71 Quoted in Isaac Deutscher, *The Unfinished Revoltion* (Oxford, 1967), p. 19.

72 *NZ* 35 (1917), 1, p. 613.

73 Karl Kautsky, *The Dictatorship of the Proletariat* (Ann Arbor, 1964), p. 63.

74 *NZ* 22 (1904), 1, p. 625.

75 Lenin, *Selected Works* Vol 1 (Moscow, 1950), Pt 2, p. 24.

76 *NZ* 35 (1917), 2, p. 12.

77 *Labour Revolution,* p. 144.

78 *Ibid.* p. 39.

79 *Demokratie oder Diktatur* (Berlin, 1918), p. 28.

80 Quoted in Peter Gilg, *Die Erneuerung des demokratischen Denkens in Wilhelminischen Deutschland* (Wiesbaden, 1965), p. 64.

81 Rosa Luxemburg, *The Russian Revolution and Leninism or Marxism* (Ann Arbor,

1962), p. 49.
82 *Ibid.* p. 66f.
83 Quoted in E. H. Carr, *The Bolshevik Revolution,* Vol 1 (London, 1966), p. 65.
84 Joseph Stalin, *Works,* Vol 1 (Moscow, 1952), p. 24.
85 *NZ* 30 (1912), 2, p. 516.
86 Trotsky, *Terrorism and Communism,* p. 16.
87 Georg Lukacs, *Geschichte und Klassenbewusstsein* (Berlin, 1968), p. 63.
88 Friedrich Naumann, *Demokratie und Kaisertum* (Berlin, 1900), p. 3.
89 *Nationalstaat, Imperialistischer Staat und Staatenbund* (Nuremberg, 1915), p. 17.
90 *Grundsätze und Forderungen der Sozialdemokratie. Erläuterungen zum Erfurter Programm* (Berlin, 1899), p. 5.
91 *Der Weg zur Macht* (Hamburg, 1909), p. 24; *Das Erfurter Programm* (Stuttgart, 1902), p. 136.
93 Bernstein to Kautsky 26 July 1924, in KA DV 525.
94 *Erinnerungen und Eröterungen* (Amsterdam, 1960), p. 214.
95 *Vermehrung und Entwicklung in Natur und Gesellschaft* (Stuttgart, 1910), p. vii.
96 *NZ* 1 (1883), p. 73.
97 *Erinnerungen,* p. 365.
98 *NZ* 3 (1885), p. 108.
99 *Vermehrung,* p. 12.
100 *Karl Marx' Ökonomische Lehren* (Stuttgart, 1908), p. 24.
101 Marx-Engels, *Selected Correspondence* (Moscow, n.d.), p. 389.
102 Werner Blumenberg (ed), *August Bebels Briefwechsel mit Karl Marx and Friedrich Engels* (The Hague, 1965), p. 228.
103 Karl Marx and Friedrich Engels, *Selected Works* (Moscow, 1962), Vol 2, p. 32f.
104 *Ibid.* Vol 1, p. 53.
105 Quoted in Bertram D. Wolfe, *Marxism. 100 Years in the Life of a Doctrine* (London, 1962), p. 152.
106 Karl Marx and Friedrich Engels, *On Britain* (Moscow, 1962), p. 361.
107 Lenin, *Against Revisionism* (Moscow, 1954), p. 385.
108 *Krieg und Demokratie* (Berlin, 1932), p. 35.
109 Marx/Engels, *Selected Works* Vol 1, p. 247.
110 Karl Marx and Friedrich Engels, *The German Ideology* (London, 1965), p. 86.
111 Quoted in T. B. Bottomore and Maximilien Rubel, *Karl Marx. Selected Writings in Sociology and Social Philosophy* (London, 1969), p. 78.
112 *Ibid.* p. 88.

113 Marx/Engels, *Selected Works* Vol 2, p. 403f.

114 *Die materialistische Geschichtsauffassung* (Berlin, 1927), Vol 1, p. 106.

115 *The Economic Doctrines of Karl Marx* (London, 1925), p. 11.

116 *Ibid.* p. 231.

117 Quoted in Helga Grebing, *History of the German Labour Movement* (London, 1969), p. 36.

118 August Bebel, *Die Frau und der Sozialismus* (Berlin, 1922), p. 508.

119 *Ibid.* p. 374.

120 Marx/Engels, *Selected Works* Vol 1, p. 454.

121 Z. A. Jordan, *The Evolution of Dialectical Materialism* (New York, 1967), p. 147.

122 Marx/Engels, *Selected Works* Vol 2, p. 387.

123 Friedrich Engels, *Anti-Dühring* (Moscow, 1962), p. 33.

124 Quoted in M. M. Bober, *Karl Marx's Interpretation of History* (New York, 1965), p. 86.

125 Lenin, *Selected Works,* Vol 1, p. 110.

126 Stalin, *Works,* Vol 1, p. 304.

127 Trotsky, *Terrorism and Communism,* p. 16.

128 Leon Trotsky, *Stalin* (London, 1969), Vol 1, p. 16.

129 Leon Trotsky, *History of The Russian Revolution* (London, 1967), Vol 2, p. 11.

130 Quoted in Irving Howe (ed), *The Basic Writings of Trotsky* (London, 1964), p. 14.

131 See Heinz Brahm, *Trotzkijs Kampf um die Nachfolge Lenins. Die ideologische Auseinandersetzung 1923-6* (Cologne, 1964), passim.

132 Hélène Carrère d'Encausse/Stuart Schram, *Marxism and Asia,* p. 81.

133 Georges Sorel, *Reflections on Violence* (London, 1967), p. 32.

134 Georges Sorel, *The Decomposition of Marxism* (London, 1961), p. 218.

135 Cf. Introduction to Bottomore and Rubel, *Karl Marx,* p. 45f.

136 Karl Korsch, *Die materialistische Geschichtsauffassung* Leipzig, 1929), p. 201.

137 Karl Korsch, *Karl Marx* (Frankfurt/Main, 1967), p. 56.

138 Korsch, *Die materialistische Geschichtsauffassung* p. 198.

139 Lukacs, *Geschichte und Klassenbewusstsein,* p. 119.

140 Sorel, *Decomposition of Marxism,* p. 252.

141 *NZ* 19 (1901), 2, p. 611.

142 David to Kautsky. Undated, in KA DXVII 346.

143 *Protokoll. . . Dresden 1903* (Berlin, 1903), p. 339.

144 *NZ* 18 (1900), 1, p. 18; *NZ* 21 (1903), 1, p. 815.

145 Lenin, *Against Revisionism,* p. 267.

146 Robert Michels, *Political Parties* (New York, 1959), p. 22.

Further reading

The following list is intended for English-language readers. Those who wish for a bibliography of Kautsky's massive work in German should consult Werner Blumenberg, *Karl Kautskys literarisches Werk* (The Hague, 1960) and the bibliography of my thesis: Richard J. Geary, *Karl Kautsky and the Development of Marxism* (Ph.D, University of Cambridge, 1971). That bibliography also includes an extensive survey of the secondary literature in French and German, as well as English. Obviously some significant German works on Kautsky have appeared since the appearance of my thesis. Among these, the most important are:

Herbert Frei, *Fabianismus und Bernsteinscher Revisionismus 1884-1900* (Berne, 1979).

W. Holzheuer, *Karl Kautskys Werk als Weltanschauung, Beitrag zur Ideologie der Sozialdemokratie vor dem ersten Weltkrieg* (Munich, 1972).

Reinhold Hünlich, *Karl Kautsky und der Marxismus der II. Internationale* (Marburg, 1981).

R. Kraus, *Die Imperialismusdebatte zwischen Vladimir I. Lenin und Karl Kautsky* (Frankfurt, 1978).

Detlef Lehnert, *Reform und Revolution in den Strategiediskussionen der klassischen Sozialdemokratie* (Bonn, 1977).

K. Mandelbaum, *Sozialdemokratie und Leninismus* (Berlin, 1974).

T. Meyer and H. Heimann (ed.), *Bernstein und der Demokratische Sozialismus* (Berlin, 1978).

Rudolf Walter, *'aber nach der Sindflut kommen wir und nur wir'* (Frankfurt/Main, 1979).

Mention should also be made of some important work in Italy, especially the essays in *Storia del marxismo contemporaneo (Annali Istituto Giangiacome Feltrinelli*, 15 (1973)) and the following:

G. Radczun, 'Il significato storico, filosofico e politico del conflitto tra Rosa Luxemburg e Karl Kautsky nel 1910', in *Rosa Luxemburg e lo sviluppo del pensiero marxista* (Milan, 1977), p. 307-14.

D. Settembrini, 'Kautskismo e Leninismo' in *L'est* (1974, 1-2, pp. 54-128.

Unfortunately the most significant and monumental study of Kautsky appears in Polish, though it is at present being translated into German. This is:

M. Waldenberg, *Myśl polityczna Karola Kautskyego w okresie sporu z rewizjonizmen (1898-1909)* (Cracow, 1970).

Works by Kautsky in English

Communism in Central Europe at the Time of the Reformation (London, 1897)
The Social Revolution (London, 1909)
The Dictatorship of the Proletariat (London, 1918)
The Guilt of William Hohenzollern (London, 1919)
The Economic Doctrines of Karl Marx (London, 1925)
The Labour Revolution (London, 1925)
Foundations of Christianity: a Study in Christian Origins (London, 1925)
Are the Jews a Race? (London, 1926)
Thomas More and his Utopia (London, 1927)
Bolshevism at a Deadlock (London, 1930)
The Class Struggle (New York, 1971)
Karl Kautsky. Selected Political Writings, ed. Patrick Goode (London, 1983)

Works by Kautsky's contemporaries in English

Vladimir Akimov, *The Second Congress of the Russian Social Democratic Party (1904)*, reproduced in Jonathan Frankel (ed.), *Vladimir Akimov on the Dilemmas of Russian Marxism* (Cambridge, 1969)
Otto Bauer, *The Austrian Revolution* (London, 1925)
August Bebel, *My Life* (London, 1912)
——, *Women and Socialism* (London, n.d.)
Eduard Bernstein, *Evolutionary Socialism* (London, 1907)
——, *My Years of Exile* (London, 1921)
Friedrich Engels, *Anti-Dühring* (Moscow, 1962)
——, *The German Revolutions* (Chicago, 1967)

Further reading

Friedrich Engels, *The Dialectics of Nature* (London, 1962)
Antonio Gramsci, *The Modern Prince and Other Writings* (London, 1957)
———, *Prison Notebooks* (London, 1971)
Rudolf Hilferding, *Financial Capital* (London, 1978)
J. S. Hobson, *Imperialism* (London, 1902)
Karl Korsch, *Marxism and Philosophy* (London, 1970)
Antonio Labriola, *Essays on the Materialist Conception of History* (London, 1966)
V. I. Lenin, *Selected Works* (Moscow, 1950)
———, *Against Revisionism* (Moscow, 1954)
———, *The State and Revolution* (Moscow, n.d.)
———, *Collected Works*, (Moscow, 1961)
———, *Essential Works*, ed. Henry M. Christian (New York, 1966)
Paul Lensch, *Three Years of World Revolution* (London, 1918)
Karl Liebknecht, *Militarism and Anti-Militarism* (Glasgow, 1917)
Georg Lukács, *History and Class Consciousness* (London, 1971)
———, *Lenin* (London, 1970)
Rosa Luxemburg, *The Crisis in German Social Democracy* (New York, 1919)
———, *The Accumulation of Capital* (London, 1963)
———, *Rosa Luxemburg Speaks*, ed. Mary Alice Walters (New York, 1970)
———, *Selected Political Writings*, ed. Robert Looker (London, 1972)
Karl Marx, *Early Writings*, ed. T. B. Bottomore (London, 1963)
———, *Early Writings*, ed. David McLellan (London, 1971)
———, *The Poverty of Philosophy* (New York, 1963)
———, *Pre-Capitalist Economic Formations* (London, 1964)
———, *Grundrisse* (London, 1973)
———, *Selected Writings in Sociology and Social Philosophy*, ed. T. B. Bottomore and Maximilien Rubel (London, 1969)
——— and Frederick Engels, *Selected Correspondence* (Moscow, n.d.)
———, *Selected Works* (Moscow, 1962)
———, *The German Ideology* (London, 1965)
———, *On Britain* (Moscow, 1962)
———, *Collected Works* (London, 1975)
Anton Pannekoek, *Lenin as Philosopher* (New York, 1948)
———, *The Way to Workers' Control* (London, 1957)

G. V. Plekhanov, *Anarchism and Socialism* (London, 1906)
———, *The Materialistic Conception of History* (London, 1940)
———, *The Role of the Individual in History* (London, 1940)
———, *Selected Philosophical Works* (Moscow, 1961)
———, *Fundamental Problems of Marxism* (London, 1969)
Philip Scheidemann, *Memoirs of a Social Democrat* (London, 1929)
Georges Sorel, *The Decomposition of Marxism* (London, 1961)
———, *Reflections on Violence* (London, 1961)
Herbert Spencer, *The Evolution of Society* (Chicago, 1967)
Joseph Stalin, *Works* (Moscow, 1952-)
Leon Trotsky, *The Revolution Betrayed* (London, 1957)
———, *Permanent Revolution and Results and Prospects* (London, 1962)
———, *Terrorism and Communism* (Ann Arbor, 1963)
———, *History of the Russian Revolution* (London, 1967)
———, *Stalin* (London, 1969)

Secondary works in English

There is such a vast literature on Marx, the history of Marxism, Lenin and the Russian Revolution that I only include below those which discuss these various topics with reference to Kautsky and his work.

ON IDEOLOGY AND IDEOLOGIES
Abraham Ascher, 'Russian Marxism and the German Revolution, 1917-1920', in *Archiv für Sozialgeschichte* (Hanover, 1966-7), pp. 391-439.
———, 'Axelrod and Kautsky', in *Slavic Review* (1967), pp. 94-112.
Sydney D. Bailey, 'The Revision of Marxism', in *The Review of Politics* (1954), pp. 452-62.
Samuel H. Baron, 'Between Marx and Lenin' in L. Labedz, *Revisionism* (London, 1962).
———, *Plekhanov. Father of Russian Marxism* (London, 1963).
———, 'Plekhanov and the Russian Revolution of 1905', in John Shelton Curtiss, *Essays in Russian and Soviet History* (Leiden, 1963).
Lelio Basso, *Rosa Luxemburg* (London, 1975).
Richard Breitmann, *German Socialism and Weimar Democracy* (North Carolina, 1981).

Serge Briscianer, *Pannekoek and the Worker's Councils* (St Louis, 1978).

J. W. Burrow, *Evolution and Society. A Study in Victorian Social Theory* (Cambridge, 1966).

Kenneth R. Calkins, *Hugo Haase* (North Carolina, 1979).

John M. Cammett, *Antonio Gramsci and the Origins of Italian Communism* (Stanford, 1969).

F. Claudin, 'Democracy and dictatorship in Lenin and Kautsky', in *New Left Review* (1978), 106, pp. 59-76.

G. D. H. Cole, *History of Socialist Though* (London, 1956).

Horace B. Davies, *Nationalism and Socialism* (New York, 1967).

Isaac Deutscher, *Trotsky* (London, 1954-63).

Milorad M. Drachkovitch, *The Revolutionary Internationals* (London, 1966).

Charles F. Elliott, '"Qui custodiat sacra?". Problems of Marxist revisionism' in *Journal of the History of Ideas* (1967), pp. 71-86.

Merle Fainsod, *International Socialism and World War* (Cambridge, Mass., 1935).

Roger Fletcher, *Revisionism and Empire* (London, 1984).

Paul Fröhlich, *Rosa Luxemburg* (London, 1940).

Peter Gay, *The Dilemma of Democratic Socialism: Eduard Bernstein's Challenge to Marx* (London, 1962).

Norman Geras, *The Legacy of Rosa Luxemburg* (London, 1976).

Israel Getzler, *Martov* (Melbourne, 1967).

Christian Gneuss, 'The Precursor: Eduard Bernstein' in Labedz, *op. cit.*

B. Gustafsson, 'A new look at Bernstein', in *Scandinavian Journal of History* (1978), 4, pp. 275-96.

L. H. Haimson, *The Russian Marxists and the Origins of Bolshevism* (Cambridge, Mass., 1955).

George Haupt, *Socialism and the Great War* (Oxford, 1972).

G. F. Hudson, *Fifty Years of Communism – Theory and Practice* (London, 1968).

H. Stuart Hughes, *Consciousness and Society* (1967).

James Joll, *The Second International* (London, 1955).

David Joravsky, *Soviet Marxism and Natural Science* (London, 1961).

Z. A. Jordan, *The Evolution of Dialectical Materialism* (New York, 1967).

John H. Kautsky, *The Political Thought of Karl Kautsky* (Ph.D., Harvard University, 1951).
——, 'Karl Kautsky', in *International Encyclopedia of the Social Sciences,* Vol 8 (1968), pp. 356-7.
Richard Kindersley, *The First Russian Revisionists* (Oxford, 1962).
Leszek Kolakowski, *Main Currents of Marxism* (Oxford, 1978).
Daniel H. Kruger, 'Hobson, Lenin and Schumpeter on Imperialism', in *Journal of the History of Ideas* (1955), 2, pp. 252-8.
L. Labedz, *Revisionism* (London, 1962).
Harry W. Laidler, *History of Socialism* (London, 1968).
Carl Landauer, *European Socialism* (Berkeley, 1959).
Warren Lerner, *Karl Radek* (Stanford, 1970).
George Lichtheim, *Marxism. A Historical and Critical Study* (London, 1964).
——, *Short History of Socialism* (London, 1970).
Vernon L. Lidtke, 'German Social Democracy and German State Socialism', in *International Review of Social History* (1964), pp. 202-25.
Albert S. Lindeman, *A History of European Socialism* (New Haven, 1983).
David McLellan, *Marxism after Marx* (London, 1979).
William Maehl, 'The triumph of nationalism in the German Socialist Party', in *Journal of Modern History* (1952), 1, pp. 15-41.
——, *August Bebel* (Philadelphia, 1980).
Harry J. Marks, 'Sources of reformism in the Social Democratic party of Germany', in *Journal of Modern History* (1939).
Patrick Mattick, 'The Marxism of Karl Korsch' in *Survey* (1964), pp. 86-97.
Gustav Mayer, *Friedrich Engels* (London, 1935).
Karl M. Meyer, *Karl Liebknecht* (Washington, 1957).
C. Wright Mill, *The Marxists* (London, 1963).
R. P. Morgan, *German Social Democrats and the First International* (Cambridge, 1965).
J. P. Nettl, *Rosa Luxemburg* (Oxford, 1966).
Fritz Nova, *Friedrich Engels* (London, 1967).
G. H. R. Parkinson, *Georg Lukács* (London, 1970).
John Plamenatz, 'Deviations from Marxism' in *Political Quarterly* (1950), 1, pp. 40-55.

Further reading

R. W. Reichard, *Kautsky and the German Social Democratic Party* (Ph.D. Harvard University, 1950).

Arthur Rosenberg, *Democracy and Socialism* (London, 1939).

Massimo Salvadori, *Karl Kautsky and the Social Revolution* (London, 1979).

W. M. Simon, *European Positivism in the Nineteenth Century* (New York, 1963).

John L. Snell, 'German Socialist reaction to Wilsonian Democracy', in *Journal of Central European Affairs* 9, 1.

———, 'The Russian Revolution and the German Social Democractic Party', in *American Slavic and East European Review* (1956), 1, pp. 339-50.

Gary P. Steenson, *Karl Kautsky 1954-1938. Marxism in the Classical Years* (Pittsburgh, 1978).

Helmut Trotnow, *Karl Liebknecht* (New York, 1984).

Z. A. B. Zeman and W. B. Scharlau, *The Merchant of Revolution. The Life of Alexander Israel Helphand (Parvus)* (London, 1965).

ON THE GERMAN LABOUR MOVEMENT

Obviously there is a massive German-language literature on this subject. Readers are advised to consult the bibliographies of Dieter Dowe and (even more comprehensive) Klaus Tenfelde, if they are interested. In English there exists, amongst others, the following:

Werner T. Angress, *Stillborn Revolution* (Printon, 1963).

A. J. Berlau, *The German Social Democratic Party 1914-1921* (New York, 1949).

Edwyn Bevan, *German Social Democracy During the War* (London, 1918).

F. L. Carsten, *Revolution in Central Europe* (London, 1972).

———, *War against War* (London, 1982).

Richard A. Comfort, *Revolutionary Hamburg* (Stanford, 1966)

Richard J. Evans (ed.), *The German Working Class* (London, 1982).

Gerald D. Feldman, *Army, Industry and Labour* (Princeton, 1966).

Ossip K. Flechtheim, 'The Role of the Communist Party', in *The Road to Dictatorship* (London, 1964).

Dick Geary, 'The German Labour Movement 1848-1919' in *European Studies Review* (July 1976).

———, 'Radicalism and the German Worker', in Richard J. Evans (ed.),

Politics and Society in Wilhelmine Germany (London, 1978).

——, 'The failure of German Labour in the Weimar Republic', in M. Dobkowski and I. Wallimann (eds.), *Towards the Holocaust* (Westport, Connecticut, 1983).

——, 'The Authoritarian state and German Social Democracy, 1871-1914', in John C. Fout (ed.), *The State and Political Parties in Imperial German* (New York, 1985).

Helga Grebing, *History of the German Labour Movement* (London, 1969).

W. Guttsmann, *The German Social Democratic Party* (London, 1981).

James W. Hulse, *The Forming of the Communist International* (Stanford, 1964).

Richard N. Hunt, *German Social Democracy* (London, 1964).

Vernon L. Lidtke, *The Outlawed Party* (Princeton, 1966).

Richard Lowenthal, 'The Bolshevisation of the Spartacus League', in *St Antony's Papers* 9 (1960), pp. 23-71.

Erich Matthias, 'Social Democracy and the power of the state', in *The Road to Dictatorship* (London, 1964).

John W. Mishark, *The Road to Revolution* (Detroit, 1967).

Allan Mitchell, *Revolution in Bavaria* (Princeton, 1966).

Wolfgang J. Mommsen, 'The German Revolution' in Richard Bessel and E. J. Feuchtwanger (eds.), *Social Change and Political Development in Weimar Germany* (London, 1981).

David Morgan, *The Socialist Left and the German Revolution* (New York, 1971).

John Moses, *Trade Unionism in Germany* (London, 1982).

J. P. Nettl, 'The German Social Democratic Party as a Political Model', in *Past and Present* (1965), pp. 65-95.

Mary Nolan, *Social Democracy and Socialism* (Cambridge, 1981).

Jean Quataert, *Reluctant Feminists in Social Democracy* (Princeton, 1979).

R. W. Reichard, 'The German working class and the Russian Revolution of 1905', in *Journal of Central European History* (1953), 2.

Eve Rosenhaft, *Beating the Fascists?* (Cambridge, 1983).

Guenter Roth, *The Social Democrats in Imperial Germany* (Totowa, N.J., 1963).

A. J. Ryder, *The German Revolution of 1918* (Cambridge, 1968).

Further reading

Carl E. Schorske, *German Social Democracy, 1905-1917* (Cambridge, Mass., 1955).

Gary P. Steenson, *'Not One Man. Not One Penny!'* (Pittsburgh, 1981).

Jürgen Tampke, *The Ruhr and Revolution* (London, 1979).

Eric Waldman, *The Spartacist Uprising* (Milwukee, 1958).

Index

Index

Korsch, Karl (German Left-Communist) 113f
Krupp von Bohlen und Halbach (German Industrialist) 2

Lamarck, Jean (evolutionary biologist) 97
Langewiesche, Dieter (historian) 11
Lassalle, Ferdinand (German Socialist) 1, 22, 75, 106
Lehnert, Detlev (historian) 1
Leipzig 4, 16
Lenin, Vladimir I. 9f, 19, 26, 30f, 52f, 56, 64, 71, 75f, 78, 85, 91, 99f, 105, 111f
Lensch, Paul (German Social Democrat) 56f
Liberalism 17, 20, 32, 35, 37, 54, 88
Lichtheim, George (historian) 42, 109
Liebknecht, Karl (German Social Democrat) 32, 58
Liebknecht, Wilhelm (German Social Democrat) 1, 47
localist trade unions 61f
London 2, 4, 5
Lukacs, Georg (Hungarian Marxist) 92, 108f, 113ff
Luxemburg, Rosa (German Marxist) 6, 9f, 18, 24f, 30, 32, 34f, 37, 39-42, 60, 62-8, 76, 84f, 88, 91, 118, 122

Magdeburg 66
Main, River 16
Mannheim 63
Marshall, T. H. (British economist) 117
Martov (Russian revolutionary) 42
Marx, Karl 1, 4f, 11, 14, 16, 18f, 21, 24, 64, 86-115

Marxism 3, 8-14, 43, 86-115
mass-strike 9, 60-72, 86
Matthias, Erich (historian) 121
Maurenbrecher, Max (German Social Democrat) 88
Mehring, Franz (German Social Democrat) 19
Michels, Robert (Sociologist) 65, 92, 122f
militarism 17, 32, 53ff, 56
Miller, Susanne (historian) 1
Millerand, Etienne Alexandre (French Socialist) 20
Mittelstand 28ff, 59 *see also* lower middle class; peasantry
Molkenbuhr, Heinrich (German Social Democrat) 55
Morgan, Roger (historian) 1
Morocco 55
Most, Johann (Austrian Anarchist) 87ff
Munich 34
Mussolini, Benito 113

Naumann, Franz (German Liberal) 92
Nazis 69
neo-Kantianism 12 *see also* ethical socialism
Nettl, Peter (historian) 35, 39f, 46
Noske, Gustav (German Social Democrat) 47
November Revolution (1918 Germany) 20, 75, 94

Owen, Robert (British Socialist) 48

Pannekoek, Anton (Dutch Socialist) 9, 12, 68, 71, 77, 92
Pareto, Vilfredo (sociologist) 109f

_*144*_